Amazing Dad

Letters from William Wilberforce to his Children

compiled and edited, with commentary,

by Stephanie Byrd

PRESS

Printed in the United States of America

ISBN 9781615798766

www.xulonpress.com

To my own amazing parents, who handwrote many insightful letters to me while I was away from home during my college years. Thanks for passing the baton.

and

to my children, Allison, Austin, and Wyatt in the words of Wilberforce to his children, "May God bless you and keep you in the narrow path that will lead you to eternal life and happiness. All else comparatively is dust on balance."
Love,
Mom (and Dad)

Acknowledgements

Special thanks to the Bodleian Library at Oxford and the Wilberforce House Museum in Hull, England for permission to use excerpts from letters in their collections.

Thanks also to the Baylor University library, for use of microfilm containing materials from the Bodleian Library and the Wilberforce House Museum.

All anecdotes and quotations not otherwise cited were drawn from the five-volume *Life of William Wilberforce*, compiled and edited by two of Wilberforce's sons, Samuel and Robert.

Much gratitude is due to scholars and historians who preserved Wilberforce's writing over the years and wrote of his life, bringing him to our attention today.

I am especially grateful to Larry Weeden for his expert editing skills. With great care and detail he corrected errors and re-worked the text for clarity and more pleasurable reading. Larry also offered helpful advice on how to transform the manuscript into a book.

I am thankful for the many friends and family who faithfully asked how the project was going and whose prayers gently prodded it on to completion.

Finally, special thanks to my dad, who graciously read multiple versions of the manuscript and offered valuable insight.

Contents

Introduction

Best known for his tireless and eventually successful efforts to abolish the British slave trade, William Wilberforce was an ardent Christian, devoted husband, and delighted father of six children. We can learn much from the life of this devout Englishman. A significant part of his life, and in his opinion perhaps the most meaningful, was his role as a parent. This facet of his life has been largely overlooked. Yet the seriousness and effectiveness with which he treated the privilege of fatherhood deserve careful consideration. Wilberforce's letters to his children reveal a remarkably winsome and comprehensive approach to equipping them to meet life's challenges.

Wilberforce was born into a wealthy merchant family in Hull, England, in 1759. His father died when William was only eight years old, leaving him well established financially. He was sent for a time to live with an aunt and uncle, who - much to his mother's chagrin - exposed him to a fervent vein of Christianity. His mother brought him home in hopes of ridding him of such "enthusiastic" religious influence, and he was from then on raised to enjoy all the niceties of middle to upper class English life. Cards, theater, and dinner parties became his usual pastimes.

Wilberforce was a bright, talented young man. He sang beautifully, and his skills at oratory were unmatched. He was sent to Cambridge, where he developed many close acquaintances, including future prime minister William Pitt. By his own admission, however, he mostly partied at Cambridge, frittering away his educational opportunities and wandering somewhat aimlessly, though successfully, into politics. He clearly had an insufficient foundation for developing a life based on lasting values.

All this changed dramatically following his "great change." In his early twenties, Wilberforce experienced either a return to the faith of his youth or a conversion – he himself did not seem to know which. Whatever occurred, his life was never the same. He returned to Parliament with a clear vision of his life's work, with the goals of ending the British slave trade and improving public morality. He developed a lifestyle of philanthropy. With diary entries keeping careful track of his time and money, he held himself accountable for how he used his resources. Most of all, and driving all the rest of his priorities, he was committed to ongoing spiritual growth. He kept a spiritual journal, spent significant time in Scripture reading, and devoted himself to prayer. Basically, he hit the ground running toward his new life goals and never looked back.

In the midst of this disciplined, active life, Wilberforce came to have a family of his own. He was nearly a confirmed bachelor before finally marrying in 1797 at the age of 38. Through a mutual friend, he became acquainted with his wife-to-be, Barbara Ann Spooner. The two exchanged letters, fell in love upon meeting in person, and were married within just a couple of months. They shared the same fervent faith and enjoyed reading together. By all accounts, their marriage was harmonious and enjoyable to both. They had six children, all within the first ten years of their marriage: William (1798), Barbara (1799), Elizabeth (1801), Robert (1802), Samuel (1805), and Henry (1807). Again, much to his delight, Wilberforce's life had been permanently altered.

Wilberforce's experiences set the stage for his understanding not only the necessity, but also the radical urgency of imparting a comprehensive Christian worldview to each of his beloved children. Deep remorse over many of his prior actions, particularly the lost educational opportunities and wasted time, had helped fuel decided changes in his own behavior, as well as a desire to share his newfound light with others. To prevent his children from repeating his mistakes, he felt a compulsion to begin sharing his guiding principles with them at a young age. His chagrinned recall of his own choices and lack of guidance seem to have steeled his resolve to take every opportunity and spare no effort in trying to steer his children toward a better path.

Wilberforce's children grew up not only hearing his beliefs, but most importantly, seeing them lived out. Their father endeavored to model the precepts he taught. Wilberforce seemed to understand intuitively that while his words were important, his complementary actions were more so – that more would be *caught* than *taught* – if his sons and daughters were to adopt these foundational truths as their own guides for life. The manner in which Wilberforce lived out his faith was critical. A parent's lack of authentic faith leads children to reject as adults that lukewarm faith.

Wilberforce's life story, however, solidly bears out his true Christianity. We know from his writings, including a book, letters, a diary, and a spiritual journal, that he was committed to a continually maturing, vibrant, personal, biblical faith. A cursory glance at his life shows that he lived out what he claimed to believe. As a result, he had something both worthwhile and credible to pass on to his children. For any principle he communicated, examples from his own life abound.

The coherence of Wilberforce's life and beliefs is also significant. The principles by which he operated and that he sought to pass on are woven together with a common thread, an eternal perspective. His focus on eternity effectively guided everything else. The integrity of his beliefs, the way they worked together to further a higher purpose, is remarkable. There are no internal contradictions in his way of thinking. His insistence on economizing, for example, allowed him to be as benevolent as he was. In turn, his willingness to sacrifice comforts and luxuries set his attention on the joy of the life to come. Spiritual development, wise money management, and benevolence all went hand-in-hand.

Of course, an authentic faith and brilliantly integrated life are not all that's needed to raise children into spiritually healthy young adults. As Martin Luther King Jr. used to say, "Whom you would change, you must first love, and they must know that you love them." Or as the adage goes, "No one cares how much you know unless they know how much you care." This truth applies to parenting. In a recent book analyzing statistical research on parenting, George Barna concluded, "Your impact on your children's lives is proportional to the depth of the relationship you have fostered with them."[1]

Here again, Wilberforce excelled. Not only did he develop and demonstrate an authentic faith, but he also showed authentic affection for all his children. They knew without question that they were loved. Despite having six children, two girls and four boys, Wilberforce knew them as individuals. He saw their strengths and weaknesses and knew how to draw out and challenge each one. Most of all, perhaps, he genuinely enjoyed them. He delighted in their various stages of life and longed to be with them whenever they were apart for school or travel.

This kind of parenting, of course, took availability and careful attention. Although Wilberforce was an active member of Parliament for forty-five years, extending throughout the entire time he had children at home, he went to great lengths to spend time with his family. When his children were young, he exchanged his influential seat as representative for Yorkshire for a less prestigious position in order to spend more time at home. He continued to pursue what he believed to be God's special calling on his life, his work on abolition, while always giving his children's needs priority over career or ministry-related matters.

Wilberforce's letters reveal his ardent affection for his children and the depth of his relationship with them. He wrote literally hundreds upon hundreds of letters, many of which were preserved. Letters still exist today to each of his children except Barbara, probably because she remained with him at home.

Some letters were merely short notes, but most were lengthy by today's standards. In a humorous nod to his tendency toward verbosity, Wilberforce once confided in a letter to Samuel, "Your dear mother gives me her letter that I may add to it whatever my fertile genius may suggest. But I am not one of those animals that can get into a gallop within the limits of a courtyard."

Not surprisingly, Wilberforce's letters to his children covered a variety of topics. Some of the letters address mundane matters. Wilberforce once asked Samuel where he could have his firearms repaired and wondered about the price of "a pair of quite plain but good horse pistols." Naturally, the letters include bits of family news: who had been ill, requests for prayer, travel and moving plans, ordination announcements, and so on. Wilberforce also dearly enjoyed news from his children. From Samuel, for example, he wanted to hear how things were going in his parish.

In addition to being conveyors of family news and parental affection, Wilberforce's letters are replete with wise teaching. Since his children left home at a young age to pursue a formal education, he was forced to do a significant amount of parenting by way of letters. He would pass on lessons learned from his own experience and plead with his children to remember all he had taught them at home. He continually encouraged them to be of service to others and to choose their friends wisely, to be economical in their spending and keep close track of their expenditures. Wilberforce urged his children to use their time wisely rather than waste their days, to study and make good use of their educational opportunities. In the next breath, though, he would remind them never to allow schoolwork to take the place of personal devotions and prayer. He urged them to attend services on the Sabbath and to devote all their faculties to the Lord. And always, above all, came his counsel to pursue God and His ways. Wilberforce's letters are truly a fount of wisdom for the ages.

Despite the abundance of his family letters, and their often significant length, letter writing did not come easily for Wilberforce. He was not a young man when his children began departing for school. He had neither the time nor the eyesight to devote to the task. Opium prescribed for ulcerative colitis took its toll on his eyes over the years. To avoid further worsening of his eyesight, he would write glancing down only occasionally at the paper. Furthermore, Wilberforce was still a member of Parliament and actively involved in all manner of philanthropic efforts when he wrote most of these letters. He once lamented to Samuel, "It is so difficult, as in common parlance to be fairly called impossible, to find leisure sufficient for writing even a moderate letter to your nearest relative or dearest friend." Despite his limitations, Wilberforce continued writing through the last month of his life. The obstacles he overcame make all the more amazing his letter-writing feat.

This collection of excerpts from Wilberforce's letters to his children is an effort to make his words of wisdom more generally accessible. Whether used for self-analysis, as a parenting guide, or for spiritual encouragement for oneself or others, Wilberforce's sage advice is an unexpected blessing. There are too many letters to publish complete transcripts in a readable volume. Therefore, excerpts were selected and gathered by topic. For purposes of readability, punctuation and spelling are adjusted to modern sensibilities. Occasionally, some wording is slightly modified for purposes of clarity. A blessing was chosen from among his many letter closings to end each chapter.

Some additional explanation of the division of material is in order. As has already been noted, the very integrity of the various facets of Wilberforce's life is the key to understanding him and his approach to parenthood. It is essential to see how the overarching theme of an eternal perspective reaches across all areas of his life. Categorizing the different areas is problematic, particularly setting apart spiritual development, which takes precedence over and permeates all other aspects. As Booker T. Washington observed, "Our religion must not alone be the concern of the emotions, but must be woven into the warp and woof of our everyday life."[2] Suffice it to say, the chapter divisions are merely an item of convenience, a way of organizing the material and breaking it down into manageable parts. Despite the somewhat artificial categories, it should be obvious that the different topics blend together and that a strong spiritual element pervades them all.

Wilberforce's approach to training children "in the way they should go" is as relevant in our day as it was in his. The following chapters share, in his own words, Wilberforce's principles for being a "real Christian" and for maximizing one's availability and talents for God's usefulness and glory.

Chapter 1

Keeping First Things First: Education and Career

I had far rather that you should be a true Christian than a learned man, but I wish you to become the latter through the influence of the former.

William Wilberforce in a letter to his son Samuel, 1823

Chapter 1

Keeping First Things First: Education and Career

I had far rather that you should be a true Christian than a learned man, but I wish you to become the latter through the influence of the former.

William Wilberforce in a letter to his son Samuel, 1823

Developing a truly Christian approach to education is no simple matter. As with any good endeavor, even the best intentions can become distorted in countless ways. Temptations abound to use knowledge for less than noble purposes, if not for outright evil. As has been said, goodness without knowledge is weak, but knowledge without goodness is dangerous.

Addressing the proper motivation for education, Saint Bernard of Clairvaux wrote in the twelfth century, "Some want knowledge for the sole purpose of knowing, and this is unseemly curiosity. Some seek knowledge in order to be known themselves; this is unseemly vanity. And there are also those who seek knowledge in order to sell their knowledge, for example for money or for honors; this is unseemly quest for gain. But there are also those who seek knowledge in order to edify, and this is charity. And there are those who seek knowledge in order to be edified, and this is prudence."

Whether or not Wilberforce ever read these words, he certainly understood and embraced those ideas. He was of the decided opinion that life was not to be wasted pursuing knowledge that merely puffs up the ego. Nor were academic pursuits meant to be just another way to achieve recognition and honor or to gain entry into a profitable profession. Education was to be pursued in order to improve innate, God-given mental faculties for the purposes of knowing God and building up His kingdom for His glory.

Wilberforce's insight allowed him to develop wise, balanced principles with regard to intellectual endeavors. He applied these to his own life, as well as to his children's. His remarkable discernment came only after his adult conversion, however. His own educational and professional experience, much to his later chagrin, got off to a dubious start.

From an early age, Wilberforce stood out among his peers as a bright and talented student. A sharp mind and natural eloquence served him well. By the time he arrived at Cambridge, however, he was interested primarily in advancing his social standing. Wilberforce idled away most of his time at university pursuing various forms of entertainment. He often had friends in his room until late at night, leaving little time for study. If any students were engaged in frivolity, Wilberforce was sure to be in their midst. Not long after his Cambridge years, though, he developed a true appreciation for learning.

Following his adult conversion or renewal of his Christian faith, Wilberforce immediately embarked on what he termed his second education: the self-guided, informal version that became a lifelong pursuit. Books became his constant companions. When he was not able to read to himself due to failing eyesight, he employed someone to read to him. He educated himself on topics left out of his formal education and set about building a personal library. Puritan writers such as Baxter and Owen were among his favorites. He also enjoyed the French mystics Fenelon and Pascal. These authors shaped his thinking and inspired him to develop a deeper and stronger faith.

This newfound realization of the value of education to the Christian life, combined with a desire to dedicate the remainder of his life to serving God, led him to question his career path. He struggled mightily with the decision of whether to remain in Parliament or go into full-time "ministry." Wilberforce was prepared to give up his seat now that his vision, priorities, and ultimate purpose in life had been clarified. He had previously been comfortable pursuing his own advancement, and he truly enjoyed involvement and leadership in political affairs. However, he now felt that his primary obligation was to be about the Lord's work. He wanted to bring glory to God in all he did and tell others of his newfound faith.

John Newton, the former slave ship captain and renowned evangelical pastor who had become Wilberforce's spiritual mentor, played a significant role in convincing Wilberforce to remain in Parliament. So too did William Pitt, Wilberforce's close friend and prime minister of England. They persuaded him to use his position there in service to God.[3] Newton believed that Wilberforce had a unique role to fulfill in the political arena. As he stated, "You are not only a representative for Yorkshire, you have the far greater honor of being a representative for the Lord, in a place where many know Him not."[4] So Wilberforce continued in Parliament, albeit with a radically different motivation. He replaced his own agenda with a mission he believed was given to him by God. As he recorded in his diary at age twenty-eight, "God Almighty has set before me two great objects, the suppression of the Slave Trade and the reformation of manners." He then doggedly commenced on these daunting works, ultimately to great ends.

Wilberforce's "before" and "after" conversion experiences undoubtedly influenced his approach to his children's education and the advice he gave them on selecting a career. He spared no effort or expense in educating them.

He procured Christian tutors when they were young and sent them off to prestigious schools as they grew older. He frequently admonished his children to use their time wisely and make the most of their opportunities. He saw the educational process as an opportunity for character development and encouraged self-discipline, perseverance, and commitment. He expected his older children to be good role models for their siblings.

Happily, most of Wilberforce's children seem to have responded well to their father's passion for learning. His oldest son attended Cambridge, and the younger three sons continued their formal education at Oxford. Elizabeth, though limited by her gender in pursuing formal education, remained an avid and critical reader, much to her father's delight.

Wilberforce's letters written to his children while they were away at school reflect the remorse of a parent who wasted a significant part of his own educational opportunity. He wanted desperately for them to benefit from their opportunities. He addressed this concern directly and firmly with a son whose teacher had reported a lack of effort.

> I perceive pretty clearly that it is their [his tutors'] opinion that you are idling away your time. Let me earnestly conjure you to rouse yourself and in good earnest to set to work.

Wilberforce then immediately explained his reason for encouraging his son to study and stop wasting time. It wasn't about achieving a particular score or class rank; rather, the point was the responsible use of time. It is a notion more of stewardship than of competition or achievement.

> In saying this, however, I will add what I stated to your brother a little before he took his degree – that whatever place he should occupy, I should be satisfied because I was convinced he had been employing his time properly.

> All I am now contending for is that my dear Samuel may at least endeavor to do his school business with a recollection of his Savior and a wish to please Him.... Whatever you do, do to the glory of God.

Time and again, in letter after letter, Wilberforce assured his children that he was not overly concerned with grades or rank. He loved his children regardless of their academic success or failure and wanted to be sure they understood the unconditional nature of his love. He did not want them to be burdened by the need to impress their father with a top academic ranking. He simply valued education and wanted them to make good use of their time.

> As to your brother's approaching trial [upcoming exams], I am much less anxious about the result than might be expected considering my warm affection for him and the value I set on learning. But I am satisfied because I am sure he has been employing his time well. There is often much of what we improperly call chance in the result of

public examinations. But Robert's station [class rank] may be easy as far as I am concerned, though I certainly should rejoice in his success.

You have been employing your time diligently, and though I certainly wish you a full measure of success, I shall be well satisfied if you fail somewhat of that achievement.

I will frankly assure you that I am far less interested than you seem to suppose in your obtaining the distinction you mention. The manner in which you have been spending your time and employing the opportunities which a Gracious Providence has afforded you of acquiring knowledge, of improving your faculties, and qualifying yourself for discharging hereafter the active duties of life, will not, I assure you, be lost, though you should fail of being as high as you might wish on the examination. I do not deny that any honor you may obtain by worthy efforts will be gratifying to me. But I am much more desirous that you should deserve credit than that you should obtain a triumph over your competitors. Above all, my dear boy, I am thankful for motives which, I trust, prompt your exertions, the desire of pleasing God and of improving the talents which His goodness has committed to your stewardship. Again let me assure you whatever be your station on your examination paper, I shall be satisfied.

As much as Wilberforce valued learning, he understood that it must always be superceded by the far more important privilege of knowing, loving, and following God. He urged his children never to sacrifice daily time with God in prayer and Scripture in order to further their studies. The trade would be a loss, he knew. A proper education pursued for the right reasons would always be of good use. Education, however, was neither an ultimate good in and of itself nor the ultimate solution to any problem.

Therefore, he urged his children toward the far greater prize of eternity even in the midst of their academic pursuits. His words must surely have gone far in helping them keep a proper perspective.

> There is another wish for you far more ardently felt than any that respects your reputation, especially your comparative reputation as a scholar. I need not say it is that you may be a real Christian. What I value much more is your disposition and behavior.
>
> You will not blame a Father's anxiety for you, that while you are so meritoriously denying yourself pleasures which you would gladly partake and setting yourself doggedly to study, you should not grow remiss in the pursuit of the one thing needful. Different people are subject to different temptations. For my own part, there is no situation in which I am so apt to grow slack in running the heavenly race, as when I am engaged in study earnestly. Keep this in mind and remember the supreme importance of the one thing needful. I had far rather see you unlearned than learned from the impulse of

the love of human estimation as the main principle.

You are returned to your studies, I trust, with renewed vigor. While these are prosecuted with ardor, let me express my hopes that you are pressing forward with still greater alacrity in the pursuit of a still more glorious prize. How lukewarmly shall we hereafter think we have pushed forward in this heavenly race compared with the agony of earnestness which the value of the interests at stake might naturally inspire.

I am quite satisfied with the diligence and zeal with which you are prosecuting your studies. But let me earnestly entreat you not to forget that there are claims and interests of a still higher order. And I hope my dear Robert will see to it that these are not neglected. There is always danger, lest students should abridge the time they ought to allot to prayer. If they were addicting themselves to vice or even to pleasure, their consciences would clamor and reproach them. But when you are employing your mind and time on such legitimate objects, there is always cause for apprehension lest private prayer especially should either be contracted or be performed coldly and without due deliberation and fervor.

I beg you to keep an account of the amount of time which you devote to real study. I hope that amidst your various studies you will not forget to read daily some of the Holy Scriptures.

I hope you are steadily adhering to your determination of studying a given number of hours daily when in health, and even more that you do not neglect the still more important duty of private devotions and Scripture reading.

I am glad to find that any repugnance you may have had to diligent study is overcome. Yet, remember, your brother injured his health materially by too close application to his books, and I really should be sorry to see you push your reading to such an extreme. There is another consideration which I own gives me some anxiety. I cannot but be anxious lest you should be led to secure additional time for study by lessening the period you have been used to devote to religious exercises. I should not be honest if I were not to confess that I have sometimes been afraid that your attendance at family prayers has been affected by curtailing your morning closet engagements. Forgive a solicitude that has resulted from affectionate concern for your best interests and from the persuasion that nothing is of such importance to the wellbeing of the inner man as the not depleting our closet exercises of any part of what we have found from our own experience and also what pious men have affirmed from theirs to be requisite for maintaining the spirituality of our minds.

Wilberforce considered keeping the Sabbath to be a vital part of spiritual development. For his own part, he refrained from engaging in any regular business on Sundays, including writing to his absent children. He used the time to reflect on his own spiritual state and, if time permitted and the opportunity arose, to engage in acts of charity. His children were not forgotten on the Sabbath, however. They knew well, because their father told them repeatedly, that their parents dedicated a portion of their Sundays to praying specifically for all their children who were not at home. It is not surprising, then, that Wilberforce encouraged his children to attend services on the Sabbath, give their regular studies a rest, and devote Sunday afternoons to additional Scripture reading, prayer, and meditation.

> Forgive me, my dear boy, a father's solicitude who still remembers the very great pleasure he experienced from hearing of dear Robert that even on the Sunday that intervened in the midst of his exams for his degree he did not, as I believe is too commonly the case, devote the day to his academical studies, but walked by faith and tasted he should not be the loser by allotting his time to his usual Lord's day avocations.

As part of helping his children keep their academic pursuits in proper perspective, Wilberforce explained the true value of education. Wisdom lies not in the accumulation of facts but in discerning when and how to apply information learned to produce the most good. Knowledge should be used in the cause of benevolence, for example, as in Wilberforce's case, in the development of more-humane laws. He warned his children against the pursuit of knowledge solely for knowledge's sake, lest they become proud and selfish. He yearned for them to store up their treasures in heaven instead, for he knew that where their treasure was, so also would be their hearts.

> It is the more necessary for you to be on your guard against this habit of mind which, if I mistake not, a residence in the university tends to generate, of falling into that generally prevailing error of our day, that the summum bonum [greatest good] of education is knowledge. Life itself should enforce on us a different lesson. It should doubtless teach us that moral excellence is the true glory of man. The Word of God, while it asserts the same truth, points out to us how that moral excellence is to be obtained, while it cheers us by the assurance that though we can no more carry away with us the knowledge than we shall the riches we may accumulate in this world, yet the Holy and Heavenly dispositions we may acquire will awaken with us in the morning of the resurrection.

Wilberforce, wanting his sons to have the benefit of a complete formal education, went so far as to sacrifice his own financial security so they could attend premier institutions. However, he recognized the risks posed by residence at such institutions. The prevailing single-minded pursuit of academic achievement could be a distraction from spiritual development. The reigning vanity and hubris could easily gain dominance over more-desirable character traits. Wilberforce knew that his children would be tempted, just as he had been, by the intoxicating heights and freedom of university life. In a place where individual accomplishment was paramount and degrees and rankings could easily become idols, he understood they would need continual encouragement to move forward in their faith and keep their studies in proper perspective. He took it upon himself to ensure that words of wisdom flowed steadily in their direction.

> Among the many, many mercies which in such rich profusion the divine goodness has heaped upon me, there is none which I value more (except only the humble hope of being able through His undeserved mercies, through the Redeemer, to look up to God as a reconciled Father) than that of a son who has thus far sustained the fiery trial (for really it is a sort of ordeal) of the university, and of two others [referring to Robert's two younger brothers, Samuel and Henry] who are likely, I trust, to tread in his steps, his example being likely at once to promote and to facilitate their progress.

> Knowing that our universities are an ordeal to every religious and moral person, I cannot but be anxious to hear from time to time that you are passing through it without injury.

Even after his children completed their formal studies, Wilberforce encouraged them not to stop their academic progress. Formal education was just the beginning of what could be a fruitful, edifying, life-long process of learning, as he had himself discovered.

It has often been remarked (I myself may have said it to you before) that every man who is educated at all, experiences two educations; one in which he is chiefly educated by another, and a second, and by far the better, in which he is chiefly educated by himself. You have now entered that period in which the latter education is commonly carried forward. And I really believe, from what I have witnessed, you are resolutely set on prosecuting this good work with diligence, and above all with a desire to please God. One grand preparative for performing this service effectually is to know ourselves, to become acquainted with our own infirmities, both intellectual and moral, for infirmities of both sorts we all commonly have.

Although closely monitoring his children's academic progress, Wilberforce showed remarkable restraint on the matter of their career choices. This seems especially significant given his own spectacular accomplishments in his chosen field of politics. He did not push any of his children to follow in his professional footsteps. Instead, he acted as a sounding board, listening to their thoughts, allowing them to waiver before reaching a decision, and assuring them of his trust in their judgments. He desired that his children live always in service to God, regardless of the professional platform employed.

To Samuel, Wilberforce wrote,

When I last talked with you on the subject of your future profession, you appeared to hesitate between the church and the law.

Whatever may be your decision, I shall be satisfied.

Likewise, he wrote to his youngest son, Henry, in 1830, just three years before he died,

It is due to you to say that your character appears to me to have been so far established of late years, as to gratify me with the confident hope that whatever may be your profession, you will discharge its duties from Christian motives.

Given his heart for ministry, Wilberforce must have been thrilled to read his son Samuel's conclusion: "I think that if I were to choose, I should like by all means to become a clergyman that I might do my best to bring God's kingdom upon the earth, remembering the blessed promise that they who turn many to righteousness shall shine as the stars in the firmament." Wilberforce enthusiastically gave Robert and Samuel his blessing on their decisions to become members of the clergy.

What a truly dignified office is that of an ambassador for God, calling men from their debasing attachments to this world's idols and directing them to the true object of their esteem and love, the sum of all excellence and all perfection, reminding them that they are born for immortality, and urging them not to be diverted by the vanities of time and sense and the evil of bad examples, from what ought to be their grand pursuit, securing their escape from the wrath to come and their attainment of a proffered inheritance of never ending glory and happiness.

I can declare I hope with sincerity that to see you and Samuel good clergymen, in the full import of that character, would be perhaps the very greatest pleasure I could enjoy in this world and the next – and that indeed so great as no language can adequately express, would be to see you clear and eminent Christians, enjoying a large measure of heavenly grace and walking worthy of your Christian profession. And I do verily hope that my dear Robert is on his way to that blessed state.

May it please God to bless your ministerial labors with abundant success.

A gracious Providence has not only spared my life, but permitted me to see several of my dear children advancing into life, and you my dear Samuel as well as Robert, about to enter into holy orders so early that if it should please God to spare my life for about a couple of years, which to my present state of health seems by no means improbable, I may have the just and great pleasure of witnessing your performance of the sacred service of the Church. It is little in me, I mean a very ordinary proof of my preference of spiritual to earthly things, of my desiring to walk rather by faith than by sight, that I rejoice in the prospect of your becoming a clergyman rather than a lawyer, which appeared the alternative in your instance.

I account it a signal and special honor to have two sons in the sacred ministry. O may the best blessings of heaven be largely poured out on you both, that you may be the blessed instruments of bringing many from darkness to light and from the power of Satan unto God and of carrying on many a Christian from grace to grace through the power of the Holy Ghost.

And now, my dear Samuel, farewell. May God bless you and your pastoral labors. You might, I believe, have shone in political life, but you have chosen the better part. And if you can think so now when in your younger blood, much more will you become sensible of it by and by, when you look back, if God should so permit, on a long retrospect studded with records of divine blessing on your ministerial exertions.

Careful consideration of Wilberforce's letters to his children indicates a marvelously comprehensive approach to education and career. He treasured above all else – and desired that his children would as well – a vibrant relationship with the Creator and Redeemer. Any other good in life was to be pursued in service of God, not in neglect or abandonment of this first love. With a strong spiritual foundation in place, outward accomplishments were comparatively insignificant, being at most avenues for further enhancement of kingdom work. Wilberforce's words of challenge and encouragement along these lines must have been a tremendous blessing to his children as they embarked on the journeys life set before them.

May God bless you and enable you to devote to Him your various faculties and powers. This He assuredly will do if you pray to Him earnestly in the name of Jesus.

Affectionately yours,
W. Wilberforce

Chapter 2

An Essential Resource: Christian Friendship

You are now at the period of life in which your course on the ocean of life may be described by "track out." May your voyage be safe and prosperous, and may you at last enter port with a full flowing sail amid the joyful salutations of likeminded friends and relatives.

William Wilberforce, age 70, in a letter to his son Henry in 1827

Chapter 2

An Essential Resource: Christian Friendship

You are now at the period of life in which your course on the ocean of life may be described by "track out." May your voyage be safe and prosperous, and may you at last enter port with a full flowing sail amid the joyful salutations of likeminded friends and relatives.

William Wilberforce, age 70, in a letter to his son Henry in 1827

Once Wilberforce began to take his faith seriously, he gradually surrounded himself with what later became known as the Clapham Sect, so named for their common residence in the London suburb of Clapham. This brotherhood of mostly lay evangelicals, through their shared faith and vision for changing the moral climate of England, became close friends and colleagues. They encouraged and challenged one another. They prayed, worshiped, and studied together. They worked cooperatively to combat various social ills, most notably the slave trade. The majority of these men held influential positions in London, mostly in the political (five were members of Parliament), legal, and business realms.

This impressive group of committed philanthropists stands in stark contrast to Wilberforce's friends during his Cambridge days. His college acquaintances were, for the most part, a loosely affiliated group whose only apparent ideal was momentary amusement.

Wilberforce's relationship with members of the Clapham group also differed notably from the occasional social events he attended through the years. Scattered throughout his diary are recorded unusual bouts of frustration after returning from what he deemed to be a wasted evening of meaningless conversation. In contrast, he experienced tremendous delight from communing with his more likeminded friends.

Even before marriage and children, following his conversion to the evangelical Christian faith, Wilberforce wrote, "Living in town disagrees with me, I must endeavor to find Christian converse in the country." Just two days later, on Christmas Eve, John Thornton, a brother of the aunt with whom Wilberforce had lived temporarily as a child, invited him to stay with him at Clapham any time he wished. Thornton wrote, "You cannot be too wary in forming connections. The fewer new friends, perhaps, the better. I shall at any time be glad to see you here, and can quarter you, and let you be as retired as possible, and hope we shall never be on a footing of ceremony." On January 3, Wilberforce dined with the Thorntons and concluded, "I will go there as often as I dare [go] anywhere." And so began a friendship that became a community.

The Clapham group was such a unique and powerful force in Wilberforce's life that it invites consideration. The individuals involved were outstanding in their own right.

John Thornton was a successful businessman who had accumulated great wealth, from which he gave generously. Wilberforce kept a room in Thornton's house until Thornton's death in 1790. Then in 1792 he began sharing a house, also in Clapham, with Thornton's youngest son, Henry. In 1797, Wilberforce married and moved into a house on Thornton's estate. He lived there with his family until 1808, when they moved to Kensington Gore. (Wilberforce also maintained a home in London that he used as a meeting place and residence during parliamentary sessions.)

Henry Thornton, along with his two brothers, went on to become a member of Parliament. His hospitality is credited with playing a significant role in the gathering of the Clapham Sect.

John Thornton brought Henry Venn, one of the most distinguished early evangelical ministers, to Clapham in 1756. Venn's son, John Venn, later became rector of Clapham, where he served from 1792 until his death in 1813. John Venn was the chaplain, of sorts, for the Clapham group.

James Stephen was another central figure. A passionate lawyer and excellent writer, Stephen practiced law in the West Indies early in his career. Appalled by the cruelties of slavery, he forwarded information on the treatment of slaves to Wilberforce. Later he became an acclaimed lawyer in England, known for his abilities as a speaker. Stephen lived in Clapham and married Wilberforce's sister.

Zachary Macaulay was another indispensable member of the group. Macaulay lived in Clapham from 1803 to 1819 and was known as a walking encyclopedia. His friends used to joke when seeking information, "Look it up in Macaulay." In his younger years he oversaw a Jamaican estate in the West Indies. He hated the slave plantations and eventually returned to England. His sister had married a man named Thomas Babington, who connected him with Clapham. Macaulay married a student of Hannah More, a friend of Wilberforce. An exceptionally hard worker, he would listen to the rest of the group talk all evening, and at four in the morning he would begin writing, sorting through evidence, facts, and arguments. His gifts were memory and analysis.

A minister named Thomas Gisborne (a college acquaintance of Wilberforce; their friendship had been renewed over the common cause of slavery) had married Babington's sister and introduced Babington to Wilberforce. Gisborne was a shy man who kept a home at Yoxall Lodge.

Josiah Pratt was the first editor of the *Christian Observer*, though he did not last long at the task. He was a minister and one of the founders of both a missionary and a Bible society.

The India issue brought in others. John Shore, who became known as Lord Teignmouth, lived in Clapham from 1802 to 1808, after serving as Governor-General of India. Charles Grant also lived in India until he returned to England in 1790. Grant moved to Clapham in 1794 and lobbied his friends to establish Christian missionary efforts in India.

Others included: The Honorable Edward James Eliot, who lived at Clapham on Thornton's estate and married Prime Minister William Pitt's sister; Charles Elliott, who married John Venn's sister; Thomas Clarkson, an ardent abolitionist; Granville Sharp, the lawyer who won the Somerset case in 1772 making slavery illegal in England; Hannah More, who did not live in Clapham but did visit. She and her sister implemented many of the benevolent plans that Wilberforce and Thornton financed. John Newton was of course a friend of the group, as was another famous clergyman, Charles Simeon, an evangelical at Cambridge. Simeon did not live at Clapham but was close friends with those who did. When in college at Cambridge, he became friends with John Venn. Through John's father, Henry, he was drawn into the evangelical movement.

Connections among this phenomenal group continued into the next generation, which included James and George Stephen, Robert and Charles Grant, and Lord Macaulay. One of James Stephen's sons married John Venn's daughter.

This group of friends fervently believed in applying their faith to the problems in their society. Together, they made progress in their various campaigns against social ills. They used their different gifts to work in concert and spur one another on. They demonstrated the power of fellow believers working together for the common good.

They gathered in the evening in an oval library designed by William Pitt in Henry Thornton's large country home. Henry's library has been described as "curiously wainscoted with books."[5]

One would travel and return with reports from Sierra Leone, and another would prepare legal briefs. Macaulay even rode on a slave ship once to collect information on the trade. They wrote pamphlets and lobbied members of Parliament. Wilberforce, when in sufficient health, would present the findings before the House of Commons. They would gather together even on holidays, often discussing their current crusades. After a meeting of the African Institution, for example, a party would dine at Wilberforce's house to discuss the matter.

The group's missions were varied. During an economic downturn, they devised plans to help support the poor. They ensured that a chaplain would accompany criminals trans-ported to Botany Bay in Australia; formed a nonsectarian missionary society; supported schools for poor children in Clapham, Cheddar, and several other areas; and sought the abolition of dueling, lottery, and brutal sports while promoting Sabbath observance and parliamentary and penal reform.

In 1802 they established the *Christian Observer*, a journal designed to promote their evangelical views. Thornton alone wrote eighty-three articles. Macaulay served as editor for fourteen years, writing many articles himself.

Bible distribution was another shared activity. Henry Thornton spent as much as 2,000 pounds a year distributing Bibles; altogether, he gave away two-thirds of his annual income.

The group also worked to abolish the illicit slave trade that continued even after the trade was outlawed.

Given the physical, mental, and emotional rigor endured by these men and their families, the solace provided by their friendship must have been particularly meaningful. The depth of their companionship can be seen in their letters to one another. Their words are full of encouragement and no doubt sustained them during the most trying times.

Their dependence on one another is illustrated by a trip Macaulay made to France. Macaulay had traveled to Paris, no easy journey in those days, to lobby against the French slave trade. He was selected to go because he was fluent in French and knowledgeable about all matters regarding the trade. However, he could not persuade the French to end their trade. Bitterly frustrated and defeated in a cause to which he had devoted much of his life, he returned to Henry Thornton's house, where his friends gathered to greet and support him. This group was in the battle together, and they all understood the pressures and disappointments that accompanied the cause. They were uniquely suited to comfort one another during setbacks and celebrate together the victories that ultimately came.

Furthermore, their mutual support carried over into heartfelt care for one another's families. They often lived in one another's homes for extended periods. Henry Thornton died in Wilberforce's house, and Wilberforce's daughter Barbara died in Stephen's, where she had been taken for closer proximity to medical care.

A thank you note has been preserved from Wilberforce to Gisborne following a visit by Wilberforce, his wife, and three of their children: "I do not know when we have spent our time so happily as under your roof. Let us in such a world as this maintain between our families a close alliance, that by mutual aid and countenance we and they may be the better."

One of the most beautiful pictures of Clapham life is a depiction of the children running about the houses and grounds, occasionally enticing their fathers away from work to play outdoors. Clearly, family and social life flourished amidst the many charitable endeavors.[6]

From this context, Wilberforce wrote to his children when they were older, encouraging them to select and nurture their friendships carefully.

> I strongly...warn you against forming any friendship except with those whom you have

reason to believe to be true Christians. O what blessings often result from our acquaintance with those who are so.

Remember, my dearest boy, to form friendships with those only who love and serve God, and when once you have formed them, then preserve them as the most valuable of all possessions.

A principle I hold to be of first rate importance, and which I recommend to you ... is a principle on which for many years I have acted. It is that of bringing together all men who are like-minded and who may probably at some time or other combine in concert for the public good. Never omit any opportunity, my dear Samuel, of getting acquainted with any good man.

You are the son, my dearest Samuel, of parents who I can truly declare have made your eternal interests the grand object of their care, and who on this principle selecting not only your tutor but as far as possible your associates also, have endeavored to preserve you pure from all contagious influences from corrupt associates. Now, the necessities of life, if I may so express it, require that you should become in a considerable degree your own master. Now you will choose your associates for yourself, and on the choice you make in this particular much, very much will depend, much even as to what is popularly called your character, meaning the aggregate of a man's moral principles and feelings, but still more, as to your estimation by others. For the judgment which we form of others is regulated more, generally speaking, on the quality of the friends they select than on any other particular.

It would be truly wise to be looking around you, and if you should see anyone whose principles and character and manners are such as suggest the hope that he might be desirable for a friend, then to cultivate his acquaintance.

In his last years, Wilberforce wrote openly of his gratitude for the friends with which he had been blessed. The friends of his younger days opened their homes to him and Barbara when diminished finances resulted in the rental of their home and property. The Wilberforces paid extended visits to a number of friends before eventually residing with their children.

Wilberforce many times pointed out to his children the positive consequences of cultivating true friends.

A friend describing Wilberforce's social agenda and the influence it must have had on his children wrote, "They will thus gain a taste for the pleasures of Christian society, and for that very superior tone of conversation, which distinguishes their father's table and their father's fireside.... The trash, the trifles, the insipidities, that make up conversation in general, form a disgusting contrast with even the worst table-talk that one generally meets at his house.... [H]is home parties are in this respect useful schools for his children."

Wilberforce himself wrote, "Believe me on the credit of my long experience, that the Christians who wish to maintain the spiritual life in vigor and efficiency may without injury mix and associate with worldly people for the transaction of business; yet they cannot for recreation, still less for intimate friendship and society."

He also wrote, "When I was a younger man, I was tempted to make intellectual conversation my all in all, but now I can truly say that I prefer the society of the simplest person who fears God to the best company of a contrary kind."

His sons wrote, "After receiving 'a very clever and entertaining man' many years before, 'I must record the truth,' he says. 'I have seldom found myself more unspiritual, more indisposed to prayer, than after my party had left me. I could not somehow raise my mind to heavenly objects.'"

Wilberforce found out for himself the truth in Paul's words in his first letter to the Corinthians, "Do not be misled: Bad company corrupts good character".[7]

> May it please God to bless you with His choicest gifts and cause you to be beloved by God and by all good men.
>
> Affectionately yours,
> W. Wilberforce

Chapter 3

In Plenty and in Want: Financial Matters

May Christ be your portion, and in consequence may your joy be full.

William Wilberforce in a letter to his son Samuel, 1823

Chapter 3

In Plenty and in Want: Financial Matters

May Christ be your portion, and in consequence may your joy be full.

William Wilberforce in a letter to his son Samuel, 1823

For much of his life, Wilberforce knew nothing but financial abundance. As the sole surviving son of a wealthy merchant family, he was born into a comfortable, even luxurious, home. Though not a member of a socially elite family (merchants as a class could not attain the highest social status), he still had the resources to afford all the niceties of eighteenth-century English life. After his father's death, Wilberforce became, in today's terms, financially independent. Although never directly involved in his family's trading business, he drew a plentiful income. During the course of his adult life, he owned several large estates and hired full-time household help.

Most families in England lived in utter poverty. This period in British history was one of economic extremes, brought on in large measure by the effects of the Industrial Revolution.[8] The landed gentry, those who had inherited family fortunes, and, to some extent, the merchant class profited enormously from the new technology and economic expansion. As the rich prospered, however, the poor were rapidly driven deeper into poverty. One is reminded of Charles Dickens's well-known line, "It was the best of times; it was the worst of times."[9]

As it became harder for people to survive in the country, they flooded the cities to find work in factories. With the resulting overabundance of workers, wages dropped to virtually nothing. Working conditions were harsh, hazardous, and, for the most part, completely unregulated.

Cities were swamped with the sudden growth in population. Multiple families were crammed into small apartments, and many, including children, lived on the streets. Sanitary needs were not met, and public education did not exist. As might be expected in such circumstances, crime was rampant. Criminal law was harsh and proved to be only a source of more problems.[10] The death penalty was imposed for a long list of crimes. Even children could be hanged for mere theft.[11]

For the most part, members of the upper class were caught up in their dinner parties and lavish entertainment and hardly gave a thought to the misfortunes of the poor. The elite accepted the social and economic hierarchy that governed their society; they probably found great security in it.

Wilberforce, too, could have accepted the social order as it was and lived his entire life in relative luxury and ease. But he did not. He kept careful track of his spending and always lived below his means. He regularly denied himself expensive items common to his class, then applied what he had saved to meeting the needs of the poor. We know from his diary, for example, that at times he walked or took the stagecoach to avoid the expense of a chaise, and he gave away approximately a quarter of his income during his bachelor years.

These charitable habits may reflect a lesson learned in childhood. When Wilberforce was still a boy, living with his aunt and uncle after his father's death, his aunt's brother, John Thornton, gave him an unusual gift. Mr. Thornton, a wealthy businessman, presented to the young Wilberforce a significant sum of money. The gift was made under the condition that Wilberforce would in turn give some of it to the poor. In that moment, Wilberforce received a gift of far greater value than any amount of money. He carried that lesson close to his heart the rest of his life.

Wilberforce's letters to his children reveal that he expected similar behavior from them. On many occasions, he cautioned his boys to keep accurate records of their expenses while away at school. This practice would enable them, he hoped, to avoid debt. Despite his penchant for economizing, he also advised his children to be generous toward their friends. Liberality in small matters would establish a reputation for generosity, permitting frugality with regard to more significant expenditures.

Buy a little book to serve as an account book and to keep your pecuniary accounts, both receipts and expenditures, regularly and with lavish precision. Be strongly on guard against incurring any small debts with companions and then forgetting them. How glad I am that you do not run into debt. This is a very injurious practice in many ways.

Always be on the forward and generous side. The difference in a whole year would never probably amount to much, while the effect on your estimation will be of 10 times the amount. Besides I am sure I need not remind you that anyone who professes to act on Christian principles should carefully guard against bringing any discredit on them by any part of his conduct. Here also, as well as in all other instances, he will be scrutinized more closely than others and be judged by a higher standard. Yet here I should remark that I have often observed people will bear very well your being sparing on many of those occasions on which it is the general practice to be profuse and to make a display, if you can contrive to impress on them that it isn't from the want of generosity that you are economical but from your peculiar views of duty. I have found giving presents to people pleases them exceedingly and produces an impression of great liberality and purchases the right (if I may use the expression) of being, with impunity, much more moderate than common in other cases of general expenditure.

Frugality, however, was not an end in itself. The purpose of self-sacrifice was to enable greater giving to those in need. Wilberforce wrestled frequently with balancing his own expenses and the needs of others. For example, when he first arrived at his house at Kensington Gore, he wrote: "I am almost ashamed of the handsomeness of my house, my veranda, etc. I am almost uneasy about my house and furniture, lest I am spending too much money upon it, so as to curtail my charities." Wilberforce often wrote to his children on this matter, encouraging them to deny themselves some expense they could afford in order to help meet the needs of others. In this, as in all other issues, he taught them to seek instruction in Scripture and follow Christian principles.

It gives me real pleasure to believe that you are economical on principle – and it is only by being so that anyone can be duly liberal.

To you, I may say, that if I have been able to be liberal, not less before my marriage than after it, it was from denying myself many articles which persons in my own rank of life and pecuniary circumstances almost universally indulged in. When I lived a bachelor in London and wished to give away as much as possible, I saw the best way of saving money was to lessen my establishment. Therefore, though Member for Yorkshire, I kept no country house. My only residence was a smallish house in Palace Yard. My dinner and all my apparatus was less expensive than those of any people of my rank and fortune. But I always took care to maintain an appearance of hospitality, and I used to give freely dinners and suppers to members of Parliament which consumed comparatively little either of my money, or time, but which made me extremely popular.

I have a notion that there is a very foolish practice, to call it by the softest name, of spending considerable sums in pursuit of wine ... absolutely criminal. By the way, your father has left off giving claret except in some very special cases and has entirely left off several other expensive articles which are still exhibited by others of his rank.

What pleasure will a true Christian sometimes feel, in sparing himself some article which he would be glad to possess and putting the price instead into his charity purse, looking up to his Savior and in heart offering it up to His use. And really when I consider it merely in the view of the misery that may be alleviated and the tears that may be wiped away by a very little money judiciously employed, I grow ashamed of myself for not practicing more self denial, that I may apply my savings to such a purpose. Then think of the benefits to be rendered to mankind by missionary societies. How the expenditure of any given amount of time and money (for the former I estimate full as highly as the latter) can be made productive of the best effect.

I own that though those who are termed Methodists by the world do give more liberally to the distressed than others, yet that I think they do not in this duty come up to the full demands of Scripture. The great mistake that prevails as I conceive is its being thought right that all persons who are received on the footing of gentlemen are to live alike, and without economy there cannot be sufficient liberality. I own I think that even truly religious people, though they certainly give away much more in proportion to their fortunes than any other persons (generally speaking, of course), yet do not give away as much as on Christian principles they ought, and the cause is their not economizing enough in their expenditure. Without self denial every man, be his fortune what it may, will find himself unable to act as he ought in this particular. We shall see reason to be astonished that the generality of those who do fear God, and mean in the main to please Him, can give away so small a proportion of their fortunes and so little appear sensible of the obligation under which they lie to economize as much as they can for the purpose of having the funds for giving away within their power. We serve a kind Master, who will even accept the will for the deed when the deed was not in our power. But this will not be held to be the case when we can gratify all the cravings of fashion or self indulgence in even thoughtlessness or caprice.

Now all this is general doctrine. I am aware of it. I can only give you principles here. It must be for you to apply them, and if you apply them with simplicity of intention, all,

I doubt not, will be well. In this as in every other instance, let Christian principle be your guide.

Wilberforce understood that he and his family benefited more than anyone from the financial sacrifices they made. He knew his children would be better off and live happier lives if they were economical and generous. Accumulated wealth is often harmful. After all, the love of money, it has been said, is the root of all evil.

I really believe there is commonly a special blessing on the liberal, even in this life and on their children, and I hesitate not to say to you, my dear Samuel, that you will I hope possess from me what with the ordinary embodiments of a profession may afford you a comfortable competence. I am persuaded I shall leave you far more likely to be happy than if you were to inherit from me £10,000 more (and I say the same for your brothers also) the fruits of my bachelor savings. In truth it must be so if the Word of God be true, for it is full of declarations to that effect.

Toward the end of his life, with mounting family expenses and a general decline in the economy affecting his earnings, Wilberforce experienced a significant reversal of fortune. To his great credit, he managed the lack of resources as graciously as he had the earlier abundance.

I trust I scarcely need assure you that I must always wish to make you comfortable in regard to money matters, and on the other hand, that the less the cost of rendering you so, the more convenient to me. My income is much diminished within the last few years, while the expenses of my family have greatly increased. But I can truly assure you that so long as you go on well, I shall never grudge a shilling of what I make to my dear Samuel.

Now when I find my income considerably decreased on the one hand and my expenses (from my four sons) greatly increased on the other, economy must even be made parsimony, which justly construed does not in my meaning at all exclude generosity.

Wilberforce continued to urge his children to be frugal when possible, but not merely to preserve his dwindling funds. He was careful to communicate to them a wiser, more selfless reason for economizing: to be able to meet the needs of others. Furthermore, lacking abundance was no excuse for failing to give. He knew this others-centered approach was a healthier way to think about money.

I can truly say that I do not covet for my children great wealth, but I certainly want them to have enough to enable them with a profession to live in tolerable comfort. Very few persons of my fortune educate four sons at college, and William's maintenance now lies wholly on me, so that this is the period at which I feel the pressure of a family more than I shall at any future period. Yet I can sincerely declare that my wish that my children should be economical, which is quite consistent with being generous, nay as I said before I believe even necessary to it, arises far more from my conviction of the effects of economical habits on their minds and happiness, in future life, than on account of the money that will be thereby saved.

However, my dear Samuel, you are not inclined to be extravagant, and I must help you out, so long as I am able if your own income does not suffice. But for the first time in my life, this question of finance has become a subject of anxiety to me, and yet I am inaccurate in so saying; for I really never do dwell on the subject.

During the last few years of his life, Wilberforce's resources had become so limited that he was forced to rent out his home. Lacking a home of their own was not convenient, and the social stigma associated with his diminished financial position surely did not go unnoticed. However, with his usual panache, Wilberforce wrote to Samuel that their "wanderings had commenced" and proceeded to schedule lengthy visits to friends and family. Wilberforce felt the sting of not being able to entertain in his own home as he had for so many decades. Leaving behind his cherished library was particularly difficult. He found great joy, however, in residing with the friends and adult children with whom he had been blessed. He and Barbara were able to spend considerably more time with their children and grandchildren than if they had maintained their own home. For this unexpected blessing, they both were thankful.

> I find I am considerably poorer than I had supposed. But I should be ashamed were I to have any other prevailing feeling than thankfulness. I think I feel most the loss of my books. However, I assure you that I would not exchange my situation, embarrassed as it is. You cannot conceive how little time I appear to have at my own command while passing our lives in this vagarious mode. Which, however, calls forth emotions of gratitude to the Giver of all good who has raised up for me so many and so kind friends.
>
> The more frequent, more continued, and closer opportunities of witnessing your conscientious and diligent discharge of your pastoral duties, opportunities which I probably should not have enjoyed in the same degree had I still a residence of my own, more than compensate all I suffer from the want of a proper home. Indeed, there are but two particulars that I at all feel, the absence of my books and the not being able to practice hospitality, though that is a rather vulgar word for expressing my meaning, which is the pleasure of receiving those we have under our roof, joining with them more and more in family prayers, shaking hands with them, and interchanging continual mutual affection.

Toward the end of his life, Wilberforce had the insight to observe, "I can scarce understand why my life is spared so long, except it be to show that a man can be as happy without a fortune as with one." In plenty and in want, he exhibited tremendous grace and generosity of spirit. He was not driven by greed or undue concern about his financial future. The manner in which he lived communicated that while it is essential to be a good steward, there are more important concerns than financial security. The Lord provided, and Wilberforce was liberated to concentrate on matters of eternal consequence. His children must have benefited enormously from his rightly placed priorities on financial matters.

> May God bless and preserve you and grant you His Holy Spirit and a disposition to be willing to deny yourself whenever your Savior calls you so to do.
>
> Affectionately yours,
> W. Wilberforce

Chapter 4

"Like Pins to a Magnet": Benevolence

Good causes attached themselves to Wilberforce like pins to a magnet.[12]

John Pollock, *Wilberforce*

Chapter 4

"Like Pins to a Magnet": Benevolence

Good causes attached themselves to Wilberforce like pins to a magnet.[12]

John Pollock, *Wilberforce*

The name William Wilberforce has become synonymous with benevolence. From his early twenties onward, Wilberforce ordered his life so that he could be involved in all sorts of philanthropic endeavors. In the broadest possible sense, from sacrificial giving to personal investment of time, influence, and energy, Wilberforce developed a lifestyle of benevolence. His life seemed the very embodiment of a serious response to the biblical admonition, "Anyone, then, who knows the good he ought to do and doesn't do it, sins."[13]

Wilberforce is widely known for his tireless efforts in the cause of abolition. For years he risked life and health to lead the grueling battle in Parliament to abolish the British slave trade. The struggle did not end with doing away with the trade by law. For years afterward, Wilberforce and his companions worked to stop the illegal trade of slaves. Then he took on the international community, persevering in the cause until other nations were forced to halt their slave trade. Finally, Wilberforce worked with American abolitionists to end slavery itself in the British colonies.

Having played an integral role in such a demanding political battle, Wilberforce could have been excused for retreating from other public matters and tending to his considerable personal and family responsibilities. But he did not.

As was described in the previous chapter, life in England for the working class left much to be desired. Virtually every aspect of society cried out for reform. There were no public schools, food stamps, or county health departments. There was no oversight of factory work conditions or limitation of child labor. Punishments for minor crimes were outrageous, corruption in the political system was widespread, and the civil rights of religious minorities were violated with impunity.

Wilberforce and like-minded reformers took on all these issues and more. They worked with the "liberals" of their day to improve criminal law, child labor law, and work conditions, particularly with regard to cotton mills and chimney sweeps. Wilberforce helped lead the charge for parliamentary reform, hoping to make it more difficult for a candidate to buy his way into office. He also voted to allow Catholics to become members of Parliament. Each of these efforts represented a great deal of time and energy, not to mention political risk. However, they all played a role in improving the lives of thousands of people.

Wilberforce's benevolence was not limited to needs within his own country. He was appalled by descriptions he read of conditions in Haiti and India. He started and chaired committees, wrote letters, recruited chaplains - whatever he could do to minister to those in need in foreign lands.

Most striking, though, was Wilberforce's personal generosity. His love for people and his commitment to meeting their needs shine through far beyond his involvement in the political domain.

Wilberforce was open-handed with the resources God had allowed him to accumulate. He saw to it, for example, that Charles Wesley's widow was provided for until her death in 1822. Over the years, he also dedicated a significant sum for the education of promising young men who otherwise would not have been able to afford a formal education. During an economic recession in the early 1800s, he reportedly gave away three thousand pounds more than his income that year. He sent money to local clergymen for distribution among the poor. His prayer in giving was always, "O Lord, guide me right."

A particularly inspiring story of Wilberforce's benevolent spirit unfolded while he was visiting a friend, Hannah More, and her sister

Martha in August 1789 at Cowslip Green. Martha recorded the incident in her journal. The sisters had insisted that Wilberforce take a day to enjoy the cliffs of Cheddar, an area known for its great natural beauty. When he returned, Martha asked how he had found the cliffs and was met with a surprising response. They "were very fine," according to Wilberforce, "but the poverty and distress of the people was dreadful." According to Martha, he then went to his room to be alone for a while. At supper he excitedly implored, "Miss Hannah More, something must be done for Cheddar." He described his discoveries about the area and its residents – no clergy lived there, and no industry existed to provide jobs. Wilberforce and the Mores stayed up late that evening discussing what might be done, and in the end Wilberforce told Hannah, "If you will be at the trouble, I will be at the expense."

Wilberforce also described the experience in his diary. He intended to read and picnic in the scenic country "but could not get rid of the people." So he "had some talk with the people." He observed how grateful they were for anything he gave them and determined to do more.

One of the first goals was to find a good minister who would live there, preferably one who was married. Wilberforce sent books to Hannah according to her requests, and she began to establish schools.

Over the years Wilberforce would go back to visit Cheddar with the Mores. He was delighted to see people, both young and old, turning to God. "Near a thousand children in all. One mere child had brought all his father's household to family prayers."

The ministry at Cheddar continued into the next generation. Children who had attended the schools in their early years were now sending their own children. Greatly pleased, Wilberforce wrote to the Mores, "So I trust it will continue to be for generations yet unborn; and that when you and your fellow-laborers are in the world of spirits, you will welcome into the blessed society troop after troop, in long succession, of those who can trace up the work of God in their hearts to the ladies at Cheddar."

Even more phenomenal than his financial contributions, as significant as they were, was his personal involvement in the lives of those in need. Wilberforce allowed interruptions to his parliamentary business to hear the needs of people who came to him with their problems. According to his sons, "He gave way ... to these interruptions on principle." In his own words, "It appears to me that public men ... should consider it one of the duties imposed on them by Providence to receive and inquire into the case of distressed persons, who ... are naturally led to apply to them."

Lord Clarendon recorded one such instance: "I was with him once when he was preparing to make an important motion in the House of Commons. While he was most deeply engaged, a poor man called, I think his name was Simkins, who was in danger of being imprisoned for a small debt. He could find no one to be bound for him. Wilberforce did not like to become his surety without inquiry; it was contrary to a rule which he had made; but nothing could induce him to send the man away. 'His goods,' said he, 'will be sold, and the poor fellow will be totally ruined.' I believe at last, he paid the debt himself; but I remember well the interruption which it gave to his business."

Another way Wilberforce indicated his availability was his willingness to stop and visit with whomever he happened to meet while out for a walk. Early one Thursday morning, he happened upon a fourteen-year-old boy named John Russell who, according to Wilberforce, could not read and apparently knew nothing about the Lord. "May this meeting be for good," Wilberforce later wrote.

Wilberforce also engaged in prison ministry of sorts. He once agreed to meet with a man about to be executed. Another time he sent to a man in prison a copy of one of his favorite books, Philip Doddridge's *Rise and Progress*, which he often credited as being the means of his own salvation. He then ensured that a clergyman would follow up with a personal visit.

Nor did Wilberforce shirk responsibility when situations were dire or even distasteful. Once when staying at a friend's house, seeing that no one else was visiting a sick and dying servant, he took on the job himself. For the length of his stay, he paid a visit each day to this unknown servant. He also cared for a friend's widow while she was dying. He helped her write a will, ensuring that her nine children would have good guardians, as she lay dying on a couch in his home.

It would be difficult to overstate the variety and number of causes to which Wilberforce devoted attention and funds. His friend Hannah More once wrote of his dining room's resembling Noah's ark due to its dizzying array of vastly differing visitors.

In Wilberforce's letters to his children, he commissioned them to follow suit.

> May it please God to grant you an abundant, continually increasing measure of His heavenly grace; and if He sees good, may He render you a blessing to your fellow creatures and an honor to your family.

> You cannot conceive with what pleasure I look forward to the time when you will be able to engage in plans for the improvement and happiness of your fellow creatures, especially for the promotion of their best interests.

> I cannot help expressing the hope I often fondly cherish that my dear Robert will resolutely adhere to the practice of devoting the whole of his Sundays to spiritual and invisible objects or to pious and benevolent occupations. I am persuaded that a special blessing will reward your so doing.... It is very right where we can, to find some way of doing good on Sunday, visiting the sick, instructing the ignorant, comforting the afflicted, performing acts of kindness or of service to friends – all these may very properly occupy a part of our time, especially after we are satiated with reading or tired of solitude.

He recommended charity as an antidote to low spirits.

> Let me advise you, my dear child, whenever you do fear anything of that solitariness of spirit of which you speak, to endeavor to find an antidote for it in prayer. There is often much of bodily nervousness in it. I am ashamed to acknowledge that I am sometimes conscious of it myself. Another method which I would recommend to you for getting the better of it is to engage in some active exertion, teaching some child, instructing some servant, comforting some poor sufferer from poverty and sickness.

He urged his children to dedicate their lives in service to the Lord.

> May my dearest boy be enabled henceforth to live habitually under the impression that he is not his own, having been purchased by his Savior at the price of His own precious blood and being therefore bound to devote all his faculties and powers to that Savior's service according to the apostle's injunction, Whatever ye do in word or deed, do all in the name of the Lord Jesus, giving thanks to God the Father through Him, and also to that text, "Whether we live, we live unto the Lord, or whether we die, we die unto the Lord."

Wilberforce encouraged his children to take responsibility for the advantages with which they had been blessed. God did not need them in order to accomplish His will, but it would be a privilege to be used for His purposes.

> You have enjoyed and still enjoy many advantages for which you are responsible.
>
> But God can be at no loss for instruments to effect His purposes of beneficence, a truth we are apt sometimes to forget when our schemes for the benefit of mankind are defeated, or when we are in danger of being interrupted in the progress or completion of any good work we have in hand. The Almighty can always raise up agents for the accomplishment of His own purposes.
>
> I daily pray to God to enable me to be a less unprofitable servant than, to my great disquiet, I assure you I now am. And do you, my dearest boy, join your prayer to mine that I may be enabled to employ what may yet remain to me of bodily and mental efficiency in being of some service to my fellow creatures. Would I were a less unprofitable servant. I trust my dear boy you pray for me, as assuredly I do for you.

One of Wilberforce's last philanthropic efforts was the establishment of a chapel at Mill Hill, for which he raised the funds. In a letter to Hannah More he explained, "It will doubtless be an expensive matter, but … I could not lay my head on my pillow with a quiet conscience, if I were not to have done my best to secure for all my poor neighbors the blessings of Christian instruction, and I hope of pastoral care, that long after I am dead and gone, some good man or other will be endeavoring to bring perishing souls to the great Physician. Again, the effects of the attention which I hope any occupant of the intended chapel will pay to the education of the children of the neighborhood weighs powerfully with me." A few days after his death, the doors of St. Paul's Chapel at Mill Hill were opened.

May God bless you and make you a blessing to many hereafter.

Affectionately yours,
W. Wilberforce

Chapter 5

A Heart of Wisdom: Realization That Time Is Short

*Teach us to number our days aright, that
we may gain a heart of wisdom.*

Moses, Psalm 90:12

Chapter 5

A Heart of Wisdom: Realization That Time Is Short

*Teach us to number our days aright, that
we may gain a heart of wisdom.*

Moses, Psalm 90:12

Wilberforce early became acquainted with death. When he was only eight years old, his fourteen-year-old sister died. Less than a year later, his father became ill and passed away. Later, his younger sister died. In a family of four children, Wilberforce was one of only two who survived to adulthood.

Wilberforce himself was never in particularly good health. He was not a man of great physical strength or height, being only about five feet tall. He struggled to stand upright and wore a back brace to straighten and steady his frame. In addition, he suffered from ulcerative colitis throughout his life. He came close to dying when he was still young during a particularly debilitating bout of colitis. To make matters worse, he was prescribed opium to ease his intestinal discomfort. The opium likely caused hallucinations and significantly worsened his vision, making otherwise simple tasks, such as reading and writing, exceedingly difficult.

In addition to his own poor health, death followed Wilberforce throughout his life. Over the years, he lost innumerable friends and relatives. Of particular anguish for him were the losses of his only two daughters, Barbara and Elizabeth, both of whom succumbed to lengthy illnesses in early adulthood. Wilberforce understood that life is fragile and not to be taken for granted — that anyone's life could be lost at any time, sometimes without the slightest warning. His many brushes with death produced an unusual sobriety of thought on the subject of human mortality.

By the grace of God, Wilberforce turned neither to despair nor to a desperate attempt to cling to life in this world. Instead, he developed an eternal perspective. He rested in the peace found in knowing and trusting God and focused on being ready for his own day of summons.

His instinctual understanding that time is fleeting lent a sense of urgency to his work. Not long after his conversion to evangelicalism, Wilberforce created a time-keeping chart. Reflecting on how his time had recently been spent, he noted, "How little have I availed myself of the opportunities of usefulness which have been so abundantly afforded me! Be more diligent and watchful for the future – the night cometh when no man can work. Let this consideration quicken my exertions. Let me strive to redeem the time as one who works for eternity."[14]

Understanding the context in which he wrote lends a sense of poignancy to Wilberforce's family letters. Every passionately written farewell, he surely knew, could be the last. He never missed an opportunity to express his affection for his beloved children. He longed desperately for letters in return, once pleading with a son away at school to send a short letter each week, "even if it be a mere certificate of your existence." He knew that his children's health and wellbeing could not be assumed. His own sister, after all, had died while away at school.

It is also no wonder, then, that his letters carry such purpose and intentionality. He never wasted a chance to teach, correct, exhort, prod – whatever it took — to develop his children's character. And when it came to overtly spiritual matters, he minced no words.

Desiring to pass on to his children the wisdom he had gained regarding mortality, he addressed the subject frequently and openly. Opportunities for writing about the matter arose often. After all, Wilberforce's experience of illness and death wasn't unusual for the time. Cholera epidemics sprung up from town to town, and tuberculosis was common and virtually untreatable. Antibiotics were not yet available, so any infections could easily become fatal. Medical treatments during late eighteenth- and early nineteenth-century England seem almost barbaric now. Home remedies of varying degrees of effectiveness were common. Wilberforce, for example, once advised his son Samuel to drink milk to cure bowel discomfort.

It is not surprising, then, that a common item in Wilberforce's letters to his children was news of an acquaintance's death. More than merely passing on news, though, Wilberforce used these events as teaching opportunities. Writing of the passing of his wife's sister, he implored:

> To the youngest as well as to the oldest, be ready, for the time is to all of us not only short but uncertain. Therefore, be you ready. Your dear aunt, blessed be God, remembered her Creator in the days of her youth. She was but little if at all older than you when I first knew her. And then she made it her great business to please her Savior. The great rule for doing this practically in all the little events of the day is to be thinking of Him occasionally and trying to please Him, by not merely not doing evil but by doing good – not merely negatively trying not to be unkind, not to be disobedient, not to give pain, but trying positively to be kind, to be obedient, to give pleasure. Keep this letter by you and read it as the advice of an affectionate father who hopes if you live that you will be an honor to His name and a comfort to your family and a blessing to your fellow creatures. Or if you die, that you may go to a better world to dwell with God forever and with that Savior through whose blood alone you can obtain the pardon of your sins.

More succinctly but with the same message, he again insisted:

> The last letter from home communicated to you the death of one young friend. My present letter will convey to you the account of an event still less to be expected – that of the death of poor Mr. Blundell. O may you remember your Creator and Redeemer in the days of your youth and devote yourself to His service in your earliest years. Then, whether you live or die, all will be well.

And in a letter to Henry:

> Suppose you should be taken away, as a dear girl, your companion, was some time ago. Then how would you wish to have spent your time? Why then, far more even than if you live to be a man, you would wish to have "remembered your Creator in the days of your youth."

These letters drive home an essential point – know the Lord and serve Him well. Then you will be ready whenever your time comes. The time is short for everyone. As Paul stated, "To live is Christ. To die is gain."[15] Wilberforce once wrote to his son Henry on his birthday, hoping

> that my dear Henry may seize the opportunity afforded by the recurrence of this date [his birthday] to question himself as to his fitness to quit this world or if his life be spared, is he so employing his time and his opportunities as to be growing in fitness either to discharge the duties of life or to meet death

with serenity and hope. The means for both are the same – making God our friend by true repentance, and entirely fixing our faith and setting our hopes on the Savior (His atoning blood and prevailing intercession).

Wilberforce's belief in the eternal life of believers provided great comfort in times of loss. He was able to pass on this hope to his children:

[regarding the death of the dean of Carlisle] I have no doubt of his having gone to heaven, and therefore he is rather to be congratulated on being delivered from a body of humiliation, which was to him also a body of pain and sickness.

Wilberforce's open way of speaking about death is striking. He did not hide the reality of death or the possibility of its coming upon any of them suddenly. It might have been useless, given the frequency of death in their immediate family. Nonetheless, Wilberforce demonstrated remarkable courage in addressing with his children their own mortality. In the face of what might be depressing news, he cast a vision of a meaningful life and death. Where others might find futility, he proclaimed hope for a joyful, everlasting future:

[news regarding the sudden death of Wilberforce's friend] O may you and I be as well prepared when our last hour shall arrive. How little did we expect some years ago that dear Barbara would be taken. You may be summoned hence even before me. I hope, however, that this will not be so, but that you will be permitted to grow up and serve God and do credit to your name and family in your generation and be succeeded by children to tread in your steps. When you shall have served God in your generation, may you be taken to those blessed regions where is fullness of joy and pleasure forevermore.

To all, life is most uncertain. May my dearest Samuel be carried safely through this dangerous world and be admitted at last into that blessed world where will be fullness of joy and pleasures forevermore.

Wilberforce's "profound awareness of eternity," as one biographer described it,[16] caused him to see himself as a stranger in this world. He was intensely aware that this life would be temporary and fleeting. As he wrote in a letter to a friend upon the death of William Pitt's sister, "O my dear Muncaster, how can we go on as if present things were to last forever, when so often reminded by accidents like these 'that the fashion of this world passes away!' Every day I live I see greater reason in considering this life but as a passage to another."[17] Wilberforce constantly reminded himself and others that eternity should feature prominently in a Christian's thoughts and desires.

Wilberforce's life experience, Christian theology, and personal faith gave him a heightened appreciation for life, but also an understanding that hope extended beyond life in this world because it is not our permanent home. He looked forward to what lay ahead:

> It is right that we should abstain from all aerial castle building and remember that not only the time is short, but events uncertain. We know not what a day may bring forth. Let us therefore be doing on the day the duties of the day and then leave the future to that Gracious Being who has declared Himself faithful to His promises. This world is not our rest, and it is best for us that our schemes for the future should often be disappointed in order to teach us our true condition. For even with all the admonitions we are continually receiving of the uncertainty of all human things, we are too apt to be forming for ourselves plans of future imaginary pleasure. It is best, however, that we should accustom ourselves to submit all that concerns us to the disposal of our Heavenly Father who will never leave or forsake them that put their trust in Him. It quite rejoices me to see that you are seeking Him.

> How short a span will our whole life appear, when we look back upon it from our heavenly mansion home a thousand years hence.

> What a happy world wilt that be in which there will be no more bodily suffering or mental distress.

Wilberforce's principles upheld him even when the losses became intensely personal. On December 30, 1821, his daughter Barbara, only a young woman, died of tuberculosis. Then in 1832, just after beginning a beautiful marriage and giving birth to a baby girl, his beloved Lizzy became ill. She lingered for some time, but the imminence of her death seemed obvious to all. The pain Wilberforce experienced must have been great. Nevertheless, he wrote openly to his sons about Lizzy's condition:

> Your mother is writing to you on the subject of dear Lizzy. I own I am seriously affected though I trust there is no immediate danger. But I fear she has not strength to enable her to last long. Blessed be God, I trust she is really safe for eternity. My time must be very short, yet I should be very sorry to lose her. Dr. Palmer's view of dear Lizzy's case was from the first discouraging and has become more decidedly so. In private he added that he thought the case hopeless. My chief fears arise from my fearing that poor Lizzy has very slight stamina and that unhappily she has a sort of antipathy to all strengthening food.

> Well, we are in the hands of God. May He direct and bless us. What an unspeakable comfort it is to be permitted to cast all our cares on the Gracious Being who we are assured cares for us, who also we are told does not afflict willingly or grieve the children of men.

Lizzy died shortly before Wilberforce's own death in 1833.

Wilberforce also addressed his own mortality without reserve in other letters to his children:

According to the ordinary laws of nature, my end must be near. I cannot expect to have many more summers to pass with you, still less many, if almost any, while I continue in the enjoyment of my bodily and mental faculties in the degree in which a gracious Providence now vouchsafes to me the use of them. The time is short. I certainly, who have attained to an age much beyond that which my medical advisers thought at all probable, cannot expect to be much longer a witness of your course.

I ought to deal honestly with you; and therefore I will frankly own, that I think my present state of health to be very serious. But what cause have I for thankfulness, that at my time of life, near seventy-four years of age, and with a frame originally so weakly that the great Dr. Warren declared it was calculated to last but about 29½ years, but to continue till my advanced period without gout or stone or rheumatism or toothache or even headache. Join with me, therefore, in praising God for thus exempting me from maladies which render even the greatest part of the lives of so many healthy people seasons of such frequent suffering. Well, the time is short, even for those who are far less advanced than myself in the journey of life. It was generally that St. Paul spoke when he said, "The light is far spent, the day is at hand."

God bless you and preserve you. You little know how dear you are to your affectionate father. It affects me deeply to be now corresponding with three sons – one of them a husband and father and two of them at college. So life passes away. O may you be ever aware of the rapid flight of time and of the uncertainty of life, that whenever your summons shall be issued you may be found ready. I have been looking over some old papers til my heart is not a little affected. How year passes away after year and first one person is snatched away and then another. My mind has been the rather drawn to reflection by yesterday's having been our beloved and I confidently hope our sainted Barbara's birthday (already joined by our sweet little grandchild). How true it is, in the midst of life we are in death. Be you also ready. And then, my dearest child, then we shall never part.

Wilberforce's life and the principles he passed down to his children demonstrate that it was with good reason that Moses implored God to teach us to number our days aright. It is hard to imagine the emotional impact of such a loss-filled early experience. Although we cannot predict how such repeated, personal loss will affect the human psyche, in Wilberforce's case it surely heightened his appreciation for life. He was not inclined to take anyone's life for granted. He lived each day with the understanding, and perhaps even an anticipation, that this could be the last, lending a sense of urgency to his thoughts. He could not put off until tomorrow anything he truly cared about that could possibly be accomplished today. And as seen so beautifully in his parenting, his personal relationships took on a particular intensity of devotion and expression. His eternal perspective pervaded all of life, to great ends.

May God bless you and keep you in the narrow path that will lead you to eternal life and happiness. All else comparatively is dust on balance.

Affectionately yours,
W. Wilberforce

Chapter 6

A Cup That Runneth Over: Family Blessings

*Only one thing we ought to desire
without any reserve for our children:
that they may indeed be His.*

Barbara Wilberforce to her son Robert
on the birth of his first child, 1833

A Cup That Runneth Over: Family Blessings

Only one thing we ought to desire without any reserve for our children: that they may indeed be His.

Barbara Wilberforce to her son Robert on the birth of his first child, 1833

Early in the life of his family, Wilberforce recognized the importance of investing personally in each of his children. He married and had children later than most men of his generation, so perhaps it was a wisdom that comes with age. Or maybe it was an under-standing gleaned from the lack of parental involvement in his own life at a critical age. Whatever the inspiration, Wilberforce seemed instinctively to know that he must give his family priority over career goals and humani-tarian interests. He took genuine delight in his children, and they responded in like measure.

And he certainly recognized the significance of his responsibility in light of eternity. As the Old Testament prophet Malachi wrote, parents are charged with raising godly offspring. Wilberforce took this principle to heart.

Navigating his way through the tension between work and family took some time, though, and involved a few snags along the way. Wilberforce eagerly indulged in home life during recesses from Parliament, but during the long sessions he was able to be home only on Sundays. When his children were young, the absences were too overwhelming to sustain even passing familiarity. Once when he was home and picked up one of his young children, the child began to cry. The children's nanny explained that the boy was always afraid of strangers – a comment on his frequent and lengthy absences that pricked him to the core. This incident propelled him toward a decision on a matter that had been on his mind for some time.

When his oldest child was thirteen, Wilberforce retired from his prestigious post as representative for Yorkshire after twenty-eight years. He struggled mightily with this decision for a year or two before finally realizing that he knew what he needed to do. Giving up the Yorkshire post represented a significant step down in prestige. His friends encouraged him in the decision, however, and once the decision was made, he seemed to feel a great peace about it. As it turned out, history hardly noted the change. In truth, Wilberforce had given up none of his influence, as his character and position had long since been established, and his new role afforded significantly more time at home.

During summer recesses, Wilberforce would take off up to three months at a time to be with his family. They would walk together and discuss books they were reading. His diary entries indicate that he read Shakespeare to his kids, raced them in the garden, took them to the British Museum, organized family picnics, and played blind-man's buff with them and their friends for more than two hours at a time. At least once Wilberforce borrowed a friend's house to get away with his family for a while, calling the out-of-the-way home his "lurking hole." One of his main intentions in doing this was to make time to read to his children.

Wilberforce also invited guests from whom he hoped his children would learn. For example, a Mr. Allen was asked to dine with the family on a Saturday and perform some "philosophical and chemical" experiments for them and a friend of his children.

Sundays, even during parliamentary sessions, were spent with family. These relaxed days included family prayers, described by his sons as particularly fervent, and worship at a local church. Wilberforce and his children would sing hymns or quote verses of Scripture or poetry together in the carriage. After Sunday services, they would eat together. Afternoons often involved walking in the garden and Wilberforce reading aloud to the family.

A beautiful habit Wilberforce assumed as his children grew older was to devote Sunday afternoons to prayer for his absent children. He often wrote to them, reminding them of his Sunday prayers on their behalf. When his boys were off at school, they were assured they had not been forgotten. They knew their father was praying for them regularly, with special attention on Sundays. This must have been especially meaningful for his younger children, who had personally observed his devotion to their older siblings, when it was their turn to leave the nest.

Having invested so heartily in his children, Wilberforce experienced a natural hesitance in sending them out on their own. As he wrote to Samuel as he was heading off to Oxford,

> If ever, I say, you live ... to have a dear youth about to launch into the stormy ocean of life, you will better know my feelings and anxieties than it is possible for you at any earlier period to conceive them.

However, he enjoyed the confidence of a parent who knew he had done all he could to raise his children in the Lord. As he wrote to the same son several years later,

> You can now scarcely form an adequate idea of the pleasure that is tasted by a father and even still more by the far more tender heart of a mother on witnessing the Christian conduct of a beloved child. St. John says, I have no greater joy than to know that my children walk in the truth. This he could declare concerning his figurative children. And well therefore ought we to be able at least to desire to feel similar sensations

on witnessing the graces of our true, real children.

Wilberforce was delighted by his children's marriages and regularly wrote letters of encouragement and blessing to them and to their spouses.

My dear Samuel, I believe this is the first time I have written to you since your marriage, and I must therefore call down on you the best blessings of a gracious Providence. May the Almighty grant you and your dear wife as long a course as He sees best for you of domestic happiness. May you find in your beloved partner the solace of your cares and your alleviator of your sorrows, your fellow laborer, too, in endeavors to do good in any parish of which you may undertake the care. Thus may you become the joy and glory of your nearest relatives and a blessing to many for time and through eternity. I am ever with kindest wishes and constant prayers for both of you. – Yours and Emily's sincere and affectionate father, WW.

Often, my dear Lizzy, I have wondered how much pleasure would the event have given me had you married a man of the highest rank or of the greatest fortune but of a less established character in a religious view. Indeed, I can truly declare that I would not exchange any of my children's partners for any duke's son or any accumulator of millions.

And his delight increased almost beyond measure when he became a grandparent. This was a joy he experienced several times over.

Now when I hear with thankfulness and joy that it has pleased God to enable you to go through your trial safely, and to grant you the blessing of a healthy little girl, I must congratulate you on such an auspicious event, and I assure you that it has given your old father no little pleasure. The more indeed because from the character of your husband, as well as from your own principles, I am persuaded (blessed be God that I am warranted so to do) that your baby will be one day a blessed spirit, a child of God, and an heir of glory. I forget how it was that some little time ago I was led to look around me and to observe with my mind's eye and call around me in imagination the families the heads of which I had known in the early period of my life. And one conclusion was strongly enforced on me, that where the succeeding generations had gone, or were going on, as well as I could wish or anything like it, the blessed effect was always found to have been the effect (under God) of the mother. That general truth comforts my heart and enables me to look on the little one that is committed to your care with humble but confiding joy as well as gratitude.

May our Heavenly Father graciously watch over you and restore you to perfect health, and may your dear infant to whose name I willingly accord, grow up to be a comfort to Mr. James and yourself and a blessing to all around her in her passage through this dangerous world, and may we both be permitted to meet her, all let us say instead of both to include Mr. James also, in a better state where all will be happiness, all holiness forever.

I cannot but wish, my dear Samuel, that you could have been present when your Mother received James's letter announcing dear Lizzy's safe delivery of a daughter. Being in a nervous state, she had waited the result with feelings of very great anxiety … a rush of mixed emotions, tenderness, and gratitude quite overpowered her. I am extremely pleased with James's letter. It breathes a spirit of piety and humility and spirituality which gives me no little gratification and excites a strong and a just persuasion that dear Lizzy has every security for happiness which true religion can fairly give. The more we dwell on the subject, the more impressive it becomes. The mere circumstance that a new immortal being is produced and committed to our keeping is a consideration of extreme moment.

Wilberforce's children and grandchildren were truly the joy of his later years.

I do long to see your sweet little girl again. She is just approaching the period of life which I have always considered as most interesting, when we may discern the first scintillations of imagination and genius, and see the bodily powers beginning to develop themselves and to present to us the buds, which will soon expand and exhibit the beautiful flowers…. I need not assure you that my prayers are and will be continually offered up to the Father of Mercies that He will be graciously pleased to bless both Emily and Agnes with a safe delivery. I hope it may please God to grant me such health and strength that I may be able to witness you and Robert taking upon you the important and serious duties of a Christian father.

Writing to Samuel from Bath, a month or two before his death, Wilberforce responded to news that Samuel's wife, Emily, was expected to give birth at any time.

[The news] naturally produces very serious emotions; yet, I trust not without a grateful impression of past blessings of a humble confidence in the fatherly loving kindness of a Gracious Providence. May your next epistle relieve our solicitude, and communicate to us the welcome tidings of your addition of another infant to your present stock.

It delights my inmost soul, my dear Samuel, to see you and Robert receiving your domestic blessings as from the hand of your Heavenly Father. Indeed, the pleasure with which I can look at both of you is the greatest pleasure of my life.

Describing a grandchild to a friend: "My wife must have told yours that this house is enlivened by a delightful infant which twaddles about most captivatingly, and begins to lisp out papa and mamma, with more than Cicero's eloquence."

As Wilberforce's health deteriorated shortly before his death, his wife, Barbara, wrote in his place to their son Robert upon the birth of a child,

> May the dear child be a blessing to you and to the world. [A friend] used to say to me on such occasions, "May the life preserved and the life given be devoted to His service who has just blessed your household." May you both be enabled to leave your child in His hands from Whom you have received him with due submission to His will.

It was with relief and satisfaction that Wilberforce returned full-time to his family after his retirement from Parliament.

> It is to me almost like a change of nature to quit Parliamentary life, all the particulars of which have been formed into habit during a course of almost 46 years.... What cause have I for thankfulness that in withdrawing from the political circle, I retire into the bosom of a family whose affectionate assiduities would be sufficient to cheer the lowest degree of poverty and depression. Praise the Lord, O my soul.

> My heart has overflowed with gratitude to the gracious Giver of all good ... far more by their being such that a Christian parent may regard them with joyful hope and with a humble confidence that they will pass through life blessings to their country, comforts to their social (and may it be also their domestic circle) in private life, their

course in this world being followed by a better portion in a better state.

I am much pleased with dear Mary's letter. It breathes a spirit of true piety and of genuine humility and gratitude that delights me in no small degree. Indeed, my feelings prompt me to say as I can with strict truth that were it now put in my power to change the partners of all my married children for others, the highest in rank or the wealthiest in fortune of any in England, I should with utter scorn reject the proposal. O the unspeakable pleasure of being able reasonably to assure oneself that our children and our children's children are training for the heavenly world! As Cowper says, "O the thought that thou are safe."

With constant wishes and prayers for your usefulness, comfort, and honor here, and for glory, honor, and immortality for you hereafter,

Affectionately yours,
W. Wilberforce

Chapter 7

A Father's Responsibility: Children's Spiritual Growth

Let us pray more earnestly and try to walk more closely as well as humbly with our God.

William Wilberforce in a letter to his son Samuel, 1830

Chapter 7

A Father's Responsibility: Children's Spiritual Growth

Let us pray more earnestly and try to walk more closely as well as humbly with our God.

William Wilberforce in a letter to his son Samuel, 1830

On his second missionary journey, in approximately A.D. 50, the apostle Paul established the first European Christian church in Philippi, in modern Greece. Years later, unable to visit the Philippian believers in person, Paul wrote that his prayer on their behalf was:

that your love may abound more and more in knowledge and depth of insight, so that you may be able to discern what is best and may be pure and blameless until the day of Christ, filled with the fruit of righteousness that comes through Jesus Christ – to the glory and praise of God[18]

In much the same way, Wilberforce longed to nurture his children even when circumstances necessitated that they be apart. Also like Paul, he seized the opportunity to write to his children concerning their spiritual wellbeing. He urged them to "work out" their salvation, to pray thoughtfully and fervently, to maintain Scripture reading and private devotions, and in all circumstances to live out of gratitude to and in dependence on Christ.

It shocked Wilberforce that many parents apparently made no effort to pass on a spiritual heritage to their children. Whether they felt they had little of value to pass on or made a faulty assumption that spiritual growth would occur naturally, it was difficult to judge. Whatever the reason, the net result, in Wilberforce's opinion, was that the adults of his generation did not fulfill their responsibility in this matter. He was convinced that the consequences would be devastating.

"Do we see that professed Christians go out of their way to instruct their children in the principles of the faith? Do they give their children reasons to believe that Christianity is true? They would be embarrassed if their children went out into the world lacking some essential knowledge or accomplishment necessary to their role in life; parents make sure that their children are taught everything they need to know about these sorts of things. But the study of Christianity has no part in their children's education; if their children have any attachment to Christianity at all, it is merely because they were born in a Christian country. When our relationship is hereditary, handed down from generation to generation, we shouldn't be surprised to see so many young people shaken by frivolous objections and irreverent quibbles with Christianity."[19]

Or as he wrote to one of his children,

> Fatal effects will probably result from our instructing our young men throughout the middle classes in every other branch of knowledge and leaving them completely uninstructed in the grounds and evidences of the divine origin of Christianity.

Wilberforce had ample reason for alarm over this failure of parental responsibility. Some three millennia earlier, Moses had foreseen this same dilemma. Deuteronomy 6 explicitly details a father's duty to teach his children the story of their spiritual heritage. The children are then to pass on this truth to their offspring. Each generation is held responsible for passing the spiritual torch to each succeeding generation. Moses further described in stark detail the dire consequences of a generational failure of this essential responsibility.

Wilberforce placed his children's spiritual growth at the top of his parenting agenda. Perhaps the lack of training from his own parents made him keenly recognize the necessity of parental guidance in this critical area of life. When Wilberforce was eight years old, his father died. Shortly thereafter, his distraught mother sent him away to live with relatives. Unbeknownst to her, the aunt and uncle who welcomed Wilberforce into their family were devout evangelical Christians under the tutelage of such influential preachers as George Whitefield and John Newton. Wilberforce quickly developed a strong attachment to his newly beloved aunt and uncle, and gradually, as well, became attracted to their evangelical faith.

Within a few years, his mother discovered to her horror that her son was turning "Methodist" and arranged for his immediate return home. (Methodism at that time was generally considered a fanatical and socially unacceptable form of Christianity.) Upon his return to Hull, he was feted with theater, cards, and all manner of frivolous gaieties to the extent that he gradually lost all the religious devotion he had once enjoyed sharing with his aunt and uncle. By the time he left for Cambridge in 1776, he was commonly perceived to be a moral, socially adept, but spiritually empty young man.

In the early years of his parliamentary career, Wilberforce's spiritual life mirrored that of the typical late eighteenth-century English gentleman. When in London, he attended services at the Essex Street chapel. The chapel's founder, Theophilus Lindsey, is remembered today as the father of modern Unitarianism.[20] The teaching there nicely complemented

Wilberforce's lifestyle. It permitted him to feel good about having attended church on the Sabbath, as well as applauded the generally moral behavior that he already exhibited. However, the teaching did not seek to influence the prevailing cultural ethos or assert itself into political and social debates. In short, this religious philosophy posed not the slightest challenge to what Wilberforce believed to be a pleasant state of affairs.

At age twenty-six, Wilberforce unexpectedly experienced a spiritual rebirth that dramatically changed the course of his life. A chance meeting with a former teacher in 1785 precipitated his adult conversion to evangelicalism.[21] The young member of Parliament had planned an excursion to France with his mother and sister and was seeking male companionship for the journey. He serendipitously ran across one of his former schoolmasters, Isaac Milner, and gladly invited him to accompany his family on their continental vacation. Milner accepted the offer, and the two shared a carriage throughout the trip. What Wilberforce did not know was that his former acquaintance, with whom he had not stayed in close contact, had recently become an evangelical. Although Milner was a new convert, he was sufficiently grounded in the faith that he could readily defend the Methodists when Wilberforce thoughtlessly remarked on their unseemly enthusiasm. The resulting amicable debate persisted throughout the remainder of the journey.

Their conversation slowly became focused on Scripture, specifically the Greek New

Testament that Milner carried with him. Milner and Wilberforce poured through Scripture, and as a result, Wilberforce gradually experienced what he would later describe as "the great change." Realizing anew, or perhaps for the first time, his sinful nature and need for salvation through Christ, he committed his heart and life to the Lord. Whether this was a conversion or a rededication to the faith of his youth is not clear. Undeniably, though, from this point on Wilberforce was a new man.

Throughout the remainder of his life, Wilberforce never lost the zeal that accompanied his "great change." He eagerly listened to challenging sermons, was an avid reader of spiritual works, and nurtured strong friendships with other evangelicals, both within the Anglican church and among Dissenters. These spiritual disciplines influenced him tremendously as he continued to mature in his faith until the end of his earthly days.

Given the seriousness with which Wilberforce approached matters of faith, it is hardly surprising that he systematically shepherded his children's spiritual development. He desired to impress upon them the truth of their immortality as early as possible. In his letters he urged them to contemplate their eternal futures.

> You are an immortal being, who must be happy or miserable forever.
>
> My dearest Samuel, I always run insensibly into a serious thought when I write to you from the heart rather than the head because

the deep interest I take in your happiness naturally leads me into thinking of your immortal concerns.

Once he had established the spiritual stakes, Wilberforce expounded on the necessity and means of salvation. He boldly pointed his children toward the saving grace of Christ.

Our hopes are founded on Jesus Christ, the only true hope.

I pray that our great Heavenly Shepherd will admit you into the number of the sheep of His pasture and guide you at last into His fold above.

It is a delightful consideration, my dearest child, that there is a gracious and tender Savior who in our sleeping as well as waking hours is watching over us for good, if we are of the number of those who look to Him habitually for consolation and peace, and such I trust will be more and more the case of my dear child.

I do hope the Holy Spirit of God has touched your heart and enabled you to remember your Creator in the days of your youth and your Redeemer and Sanctifier, too.

Remembering, perhaps, the lengthy and arduous process of self-examination that he endured as he gradually yielded to the Christian faith, he encouraged his children to "work out their salvation."

My dear Samuel, loving you as dearly as I do, it might seem strange to some thought-less people that I am glad to hear you are unhappy. But as it is about your soul, and as I think that a short unhappiness of this kind often leads to lasting happiness and peace and joy, I cannot but rejoice. I trust, my dear boy, it is the Spirit of God knocking at the door of your heart, as the Scripture expresses it, and making you feel uneasy, that you may be driven to find pardon and the sanctifying influences of the Holy Spirit, and to be made one of Christ's flock and be taken care of in this world and be delivered from hell and be taken whether sooner or later to everlasting happiness in heaven. My dear boy, I beseech you, get alone and fall on your knees, and pray as earnestly as you can to God for His sake to forgive you and to sanctify you. In short, to make you to be born again as our Savior expressed it to Nicodemus. May God bless you, my very dear boy. My heart quite melts over you.

Continually encouraging but never unduly pressing, Wilberforce was ever diligent to the spiritual state of his children. He felt that to do less was to shirk his fatherly duties.

I am concerned to learn from a confidential letter which has just reached us that you are at present in a nervous, uncomfortable state of spirits. Now my dear, my very dear boy, my advice to you in these circumstances both as a father and a friend is best conveyed in the language of a Heavenly Father who with unutterable condescension and love has assured us that He loves us better than we are beloved by our own earthly father, in proportion to the superior benevolence of His nature; ask and ye shall receive, ask whatever you need, pardon of sin, wisdom, strength, peace, love, heavenly minded-ness. Whatever you desire or need. You may say that these promises are addressed to God's children. But remember, He receives all as His children who come to Him with penitent hearts, imploring His pardoning mercies and His sanctifying grace. I do not wonder that you are afraid of taking to your-self these gracious declarations – you only thereby show that your feelings correspond with those of the Christians as described by St. Paul, who in obedience to his precept are working out their salvation with fear and trembling. What follows in that passage shows the apostle did not mean, however, that this fear was to be of a desponding, still less of a despairing character. They were to bear in mind that God worked in them out of His divine beneficence. Be of good courage, my dear boy, you are assured by our blessed Savior, Him that cometh unto me I will in no wise cast out. You wrong Him, however, by allowing a doubt of His gracious dispositions towards you to harbor in your mind. So cast yourself on the mercy of God through the atoning blood and prevailing intercession of your Savior and asking also wisdom to guide and strength to support you.... I am much better pleased than if you were care-less about your soul.

Despite the endless demands of his polit-ical career, his ceaseless work toward abol-ishing slavery, and a host of other obligations,

117

Wilberforce was amazingly sensitive to the moods and struggles of his children as they each dealt with major spiritual decisions. Furthermore, he encouraged what today might be called an "open door" policy with his children. The following excerpt amply demonstrates these points.

> Let me beg you, my dear Henry, to deal with me always as openly and confidentially as then. You may be assured of my complete secrecy.... The inconstancy and irresolution which you discover in your religious feelings and proceedings excite in you apprehensions that you are not a child of God, and it is right that they should excite such apprehensions. Yet remember, my dear boy, what I think I brought to your memory in my last letter, that we are even enjoined to work out our salvation with fear and trembling, as if it were foreseen that we should but too often have occasion in our working for dispositions, which such apprehensions as you describe must produce. I would not by any means say anything to you which should have the effect of willing you into self complacency too easily, still less would I speak peace when there was no peace.

Wilberforce understood that his children's spiritual growth would be an ongoing process. He eagerly anticipated signs of their growth, frequently urging them onward in their knowledge and love of God. He had a keen insight into the necessity for continual but gentle encouragement. His children must surely have sensed how important their spiritual wellbeing was to their father.

> Take comfort, my dear boy, and be assured that you are under the guidance of Him who has begun a good work in you and who will, I humbly trust, perform it until the day of Jesus Christ. Do not, however, relax in your efforts. Above all, in your prayers. Commit yourself to your Heavenly Father through the Mediator and then go to your day's work with an assured persuasion that all shall be well. Assuredly I believe that He will never leave you nor forsake you. Assuredly I believe that He will guide you with His counsel and at last receive you to His glory. Remember the phrase is "work out," implying there must be labor and exertion, not indolence.

> You must take great pains to prove to me that you are nine not in years only, but in head and heart and mind. Above all, my dearest Samuel, I am anxious to see decisive markers of your having begun to undergo the great change. I come again and again to look to see if it really be begun, just as a gardener walks up again and again to examine his fruit trees and see if his peaches are set, if they are swelling and becoming larger, finally if they are becoming ripe and rosy. I would willingly walk barefoot from this place to Landgate to see a clear progress of your Grand Change being begun in my dear Samuel at the end of the journey.

> I hope my dear Samuel will during his absence from his earthly father and mother look up the more earnestly to that Heavenly

Father who watches over all who put their trust in him and has given special encouragement to children to apply to Him for every needful blessing.

My very dear Samuel, I shall pour forth my earnest prayers for you tomorrow, that God would grant you His best blessings. My dear boy, whenever you feel any meltings of mind, any sorrow for sin, or any concern about your soul, do not I beg of you stifle it, or turn away your thoughts to another subject, but get alone and pray to God to hear and bless you, to take away the stony heart and substitute a heart of flesh in its place.

Although Wilberforce sought spiritual guidance from a variety of traditional and contemporary sources, his beliefs were influenced most notably by an earlier Puritan theology.[22] The Puritans lived a century before Wilberforce, but their influence was still present, primarily through their large body of writings. The writings he studied encouraged attention to providence, holy living, personal devotions, and private prayer. True to his Puritan leanings, he introduced his children to the concept of Providence, God's guidance over human affairs. He did not want them to be unaware of God's work in their lives and in the world around them.

Wilberforce urged his children to live holy lives, righteous before God and man. In a letter to Robert, he addressed the issue of attendance at the theater, a popular form of entertainment at the time. He wrote,

> I assure you, my dearest Robert, it is impossible to state too strongly the importance of keeping the mind and imagination pure. I believe many young men have been led on to ruin from the neglect of this very duty.

Aware of the depravity of mankind, Wilberforce understood the depths to which immorality might sink. Referring to a story of someone who had fallen captive to sin, he wrote to one of his children that

> the circumstances made me shudder to think into what abyss our nature might fall unless the grace of God should prevent us.

> The most effectual way in which a Christian can get the better of any particular fault is by cultivating the root of all holiness, by endeavoring to obtain a closer union with Jesus Christ, and to acquire more of that blessed Spirit instead of grieving it, which will enable him to conquer all his corruptions.

Like the Puritans, Wilberforce emphasized the value of private devotions, time spent alone in meditation and Scripture reading. He expected his children to partake in such times each morning before family prayers and breakfast. As with any spiritual discipline, private devotions were not to be legalistic in manner, an item to be checked off a list to avoid guilt. Wilberforce recognized that time alone with the Lord, seeking His heart, was the wellspring of a truly spiritual life.

My dear Samuel, attend to your private devotions. Beware of wandering thoughts. Let me beg you to be very particular about a morning time for reading and devotion. Never hurry over your devotions, still less omit them.

I have always found it useful to have two methods of reading the Bible – one intellectual and one devotional.

When our closet exercises are not such as they ought to be, our hearts and lives will not be so either. We cannot go on well without continual supplies of grace and strength from on high, and these will be withheld if our private devotions are neglected or ill performed.

Wilberforce also encouraged his children to develop a habit of self-examination. Only by taking time to reflect on their lives could they hope to improve themselves in any aspect. Further, such reflection should guide them toward more frequent thoughts of God and an alertness to the guidance of the Holy Spirit.

Self examination is an essential duty to anyone who wishes to lead the life of a Christian.

My dearest Samuel, take now and then a solitary walk and indulge in these spiritual meditations. The disposition to do this will gradually become a habit of unspeakable value. A holy, peaceful, and childlike trust in the fatherly love of our God and Savior gradually diffuses itself through the soul and takes possession of it, when we are habitually striving to walk by faith, under the influence of the Holy Spirit.

It is now your business, my dear child, to endeavor to strengthen the foundation of all Christian graces, by learning more and more habitually to live and walk by faith and not by sight, accustoming yourself to be spiritually minded. Frequent self examination is one of the means which you will find eminently useful for this end.

Perhaps most important of all, though, was prayer – primarily private prayer.

Above all things, my dearest boy, cultivate a spirit of prayer.

I find the morning the best time for my chief private prayers. The practice of pausing for a few moments before you actually begin your prayer and of realizing the presence of God is an excellent one. I find my striving to do this especially effectual in producing a sense both of contrition and of awe and of gratitude and confiding hope.

Now prayer is the very life's breath of religion, the very oxygen as poor dear Samuel would say, the vital air rather of the Christian's atmosphere. Keep a close and jealous watch here, my very dear boy, lest you should have suffered damage before you may be aware of it.

Samuel, let your religion consist much in prayer.

Prayer is the shield that wards off the darts of temptation thrown by our great enemy the devil, prayer it is that obtains for us the sword of the spirit and all the other parts of the Christian's armor. Prayer is the guide to God. Pray earnestly placing confidence entirely in God and in God alone and our boat can never wreck tossed about by the sea of trouble and temptation.

Above all, never hurry over your prayers or be unfeeling in them. Try to feel as if you saw your God and Savior.

I hope my dear Samuel attends to his private prayers. Depend on it — the state of our souls depends more on that than on anything else.

Prayer, prayer is the grand instrument for maintaining the life and power of religion in the soul. And above all things, strive that your closet exercises may not be a mere form, but that they may be really warm exercises of the affection of the soul.

Wilberforce believed that as he and his children spent time in private devotions, cultivating holiness, examining their hearts, and listening to God, they would be led toward an abiding sense of His presence. Wilberforce yearned, perhaps above all else, to be spiritually minded. He desired for his children to be so as well.

We are to live in His love and fear continually.

Remember again to walk by faith and not by sight. Remember to do all in the name of the

Lord Jesus. Bear in mind that He is always present with you, that He witnesses all your thoughts and actions.

To be carnally minded is death, but to be spiritually minded is life and peace.

... a habit of recollecting the Savior on all occasions – in short a habit of spiritual mindedness. In truth this constitutes one of the chief distinctions between nominal and real Christians.

Thus a true Christian endeavors to have the idea of his Savior continually present with him. To do his business, as the Scripture phrases it, unto the Lord and not unto men.

Later in life, Wilberforce rested in the satisfaction that his children had indeed worked out their salvation and found peace with God. As he wrote to Henry,

I bless God that I am able in reflecting on Robert and Samuel and on you also to rejoice in the humble hope that your peace is made with God and that you may justly look up to Him as to a reconciled father in Christ Jesus.

Wilberforce's approach to shepherding his children's spiritual growth was remarkably comprehensive. He grasped the concept that the single most effective way to teach his children spiritual truths was simply to model them. He practiced what he preached. Holding himself to the same accountability for practicing spiritual disciplines gave credence to his advice. His letters to his children resound with authenticity gained from his own spiritual struggles. Wilberforce was not insensitive to the earthly aspects of his children's lives. But, as the following quote attests, he always emphasized *spiritual* wellbeing as the most critical for a Christian.

> I hope I can truly say that I am still more solicitous about your spiritual than your temporal wellbeing. I do trust that you are living habitually in the fear of God and with a cordial desire of His favor. May my prayers be answered in your continual growth in grace.

O may the goodness of God bind us still more closely to Him. May we love Him still more and serve Him still better. I am ever your most affectionate father,

W. Wilberforce
July 1, 1833 (days before his death)

Chapter 8

Being a Peculiar People: Real Christianity

God was in all his thoughts.

Biographer James Stephen describing
William Wilberforce[23]

Chapter 8

Being a Peculiar People: Real Christianity

⌇⌇

God was in all his thoughts.

Biographer James Stephen describing
William Wilberforce[23]

The fundamental assumptions on which we
build our lives can easily go unnoticed. And
in our busyness, amidst all life's distractions, it
is natural to absorb the surrounding cultural
ethos without conscious thought or question.[24]
Wilberforce, however, was a keen observer
of his times. He recognized the deficiencies
and falsities of the prevailing religious and
social thought in late eighteenth- and early
nineteenth-century England. He noted that
while most people claimed to be Christians,
the lives of the vast majority did not display
Christian principles. Never given to compla-
cency, he took on a prophetic role, pointing
out flawed thinking and warning against the

inconsistent, hypocritical living that created a confusing state of affairs. He proposed a better way, teaching anyone who would listen how he thought Christianity should be lived out in the world. This warning to Christians about passivity in their faith was one of Wilberforce's major efforts. It featured centrally in his book, *A Practical View*, published in 1797.

Viewed superficially, religious life in England seemed to be alive and well. Most people attended church services each Sunday. England still considered itself a Christian nation, with the Anglican church entrenched as the official state church. English political and social leaders made frequent references to divine Providence, adhering to the general consensus that Christianity served appropriately as a foundation for political and social life. As John Pollock, a biographer of Wilberforce, noted, "Most people in Britain, whatever their personal faith or lack of it, took for granted the truth of the Christian revelation and regarded Christianity as the bedrock of national life."[25]

The attention of church members, however, had shifted from personal and corporate piety to business and social engagements. After all, there were fortunes to be made in the British trading empire, with attendant luxuries to be enjoyed. In short, the English upper class was focused narrowly on worldly success and self-contentment. As one historian noted concerning this time period, "[I]n the earlier years of George III's reign ... the upper class, and particularly the leaders of politics and fashion, were not distinguished by religious zeal or by strictness of life. The society ... had the faults and virtues of people who make the most of this world, leaving the next one to take care of itself."[26] The prevailing religion of the day was "[a] very individualist form of Protestantism ... perfectly compatible with the best sort of worldliness."[27] But as Wilberforce observed, the parts of Christianity that were not held in common with the world were less thought of and at length almost completely forgotten.[28]

This decline in spiritual vitality was as prevalent within the church as in English society at large. Despite its outward profession of Christianity, the Church of England was growing spiritually cold. Even many clergymen did not take their faith seriously. In discussing their father's concern regarding the rarity of real and meaningful faith among the English upper class, the Wilberforce sons raised a troubling, but not surprising, truth. Robert and Samuel Wilberforce explained that their father

> could not wonder that the gay and busy world [was] almost ignorant of Christianity, amidst the lukewarmness and apathy which possessed the very watchmen of the faith.... No efforts were now making to disseminate in foreign lands the light of Christ's gospel. At home a vast population was springing up around our manufactures, but there was no thought of providing for them church accommodation.... [A]ll the cords of moral obligation were relaxed as the spirit of religion slumbered.[29]

In a similar spirit, Wilberforce wrote to one of his children,

> I own I am sadly alarmed for the church. There is such a combination of noxious elements fomenting together, that I am ready to exclaim there is death in the pot. There will be, I fear, no Elisha granted to render the mess harmless. But yet I am encouraged to hope that the same gracious and longsuffering Being who would have spared Sodom for ten and Jerusalem even for one righteous man's sake, may spare us to the prayers of the many who do, I trust, sincerely sigh and cry in behalf of our proud, ungrateful land. Yet again when I consider what light we have enjoyed, what mercies we have received, and how self-sufficient and ungrateful we have been, I am again tempted to despond.

Clergy positions were generally sought by younger sons who did not inherit their fathers' businesses and fortunes. Passion for ministry was not a prerequisite. Not surprisingly, then, many clergy were not particularly dedicated to meeting the needs, religious or otherwise, of their parishioners.[30] By the early 1800s, in fact, over one-fourth of the clergy of the Church of England did not even live in their parishes.[31] Naturally, church services reflected the diluted faith of the clergy. As one scholar observed, "The typical sermon could be preached without causing offense" to anyone.[32] English Christianity had lost its unique beliefs and replaced them with prevailing cultural norms. Clearly, a significant part of religious life had been lost. It is no wonder that the late eighteenth century has been deemed the "worst phase" in the history of the Church of England.[33]

Wilberforce believed that religion had been "on the decline" in England for some time,[34] and, like other evangelicals, he was disturbed by the spiritual poverty he observed around him. In a letter to a close friend, he lamented "that thoughtlessness of God and His Providence, which so generally prevails through the upper classes of society."[35] Deeply distressed by the current state of religious affairs, he predicted even further decline in coming years. Greatly frustrated, he wrote,

> In the bulk of the community, Religion, already sunk very low, must be hastening fast to her entire dissolution. The time is fast approaching, when Christianity will be almost as openly disavowed in the language, as in fact it is already supposed to have disappeared from the condition of men. When infidelity will be held to be the necessary appendage of a man of fashion, and to believe will be deemed the indication of a feeble mind and a contracted understanding.[36]

As Wilberforce noted toward the end of his life, "The evil necessarily is, that men [are] led by various motives that influence human conduct to profess adherence to an Establishment of which the principles have little hold on their heart."[37] Many believed themselves to be Christians, he thought, but only a few understood the heart of the Christian gospel – mankind's innate sinfulness and resulting need for atonement through

Christ. All the outward signs might be in place, but without a transformed heart there was no true Christianity. As he explained, "Christianity is of two kinds, external and internal, and the former may apparently exist in due decorum, while the latter, alas! is not to be found.... But Christianity is a system of a far higher order; it requires that its throne should be set up in the heart, whence it should prompt and control all the various movements of the entire machine."[38]

Wilberforce believed that it was perhaps due to enormous economic prosperity in the upper class that the nation as a whole had become less mindful of God. As time passed, people began to forget the particularities of the Christian faith, some even losing sight of the major tenets of Christianity.[39] Wilberforce greatly lamented this new ignorance and apathy. He wrote, "Improving in almost every other branch of knowledge, we have become less and less acquainted with Christ. Among those who believe themselves to be orthodox Christians, [there can be found] a deplorable ignorance of the Religion they profess."[40]

In an attempt to prevent the continuing decline of Christian principles, Wilberforce wrote and published a book with the full title *A Practical View of the Prevailing Religious System of Professed Christians, in the Higher and Middle Classes in This Country, Contrasted with Real Christianity*. This book, which he referred to as his manifesto, was his most widely disseminated writing. Many editions followed, and because of its immense popularity, the lengthy tract was soon translated into several different languages.[41]

Wilberforce deliberated over the wisdom of writing and publishing his "manifesto" for years before actually doing so. He had reached the point where he desperately wished to express his faith to his many non-evangelical friends and acquaintances. He wanted them to have a clear understanding of his beliefs and the reasons supporting them. However, he anguished over whether such a publication would have the unintended effect of repelling his friends and preventing him from being able to talk with them about his faith. Upon the book's publication, he wrote to his mentor John Newton, "I cannot help saying, it is a great relief to my mind to have published what I may call my manifesto – to have plainly told my worldly acquaintances what I think of their system and conduct and where it must end."[42]

Knowing how Wilberforce viewed the Christianity of his day, it is understandable that he was eager to differentiate his faith from the "common orthodox system," as he called it.[43] In the *Practical View*, as well as in his other unpublished writings, he communicated clearly what he believed was wrong with the prevailing religious views.

Wilberforce was not alone in his concerns about England's spiritual state. In fact, a nation-wide, historic revival was already underway by the time he embraced Christianity as a young adult. John Wesley had brought Christianity to life for much of England's lower classes. Wesley's efforts led to what ultimately became known as Methodism. The same revival was instrumental in the development of evangelicalism in the middle and upper classes.[44]

The evangelicals reacted strongly to the worldliness and weak "Christianity" of their day. As one historian explains, "It was against this vague, undemanding concept of Christianity, which pushed God and his commandments far into the background of man's consciousness, that the Evangelicals rebelled."[45] They were greatly disturbed by what they perceived to be a state of spiritual poverty and decay in their society and church. They believed fervently in personal evangelism and hoped to change their culture by transforming individual lives. They also saw a need to act directly in the political and social realms in the name of justice and humanity on behalf of those who had no voice. Their efforts were responsible for many of the landmark social reforms, including child labor laws, prison reform, reduction in harshness of criminal and civil law, and increased protections for workers from unscrupulous employers. The net result was a marked improvement in living and working conditions for the poor.

The impact of the evangelical movement on England and many other parts of the world during the first half of the nineteenth century could hardly be overestimated. Evangelicals exerted a tremendous influence on the social and political structure of England, as well as on the Church of England itself.[46] They became actively involved in foreign missions, Bible distribution, various philanthropic activities, and, perhaps most notably, the effort to end the British slave trade. According to one British historian, between 1800 and 1860, "there was hardly an area of life which they did not touch or affect."[47]

Arguably the most significant contribution John Newton made to Wilberforce's spiritual development was his conviction that spirituality is not limited to the realm of private devotions. Newton believed that true Christianity, while based on an internal faith, should pervade every aspect of a person's life. This meant that a complete spirituality involved public action as well as private devotions. In Newton's own words, "Religion is not confined to devotional exercises, but rather consists in doing all we are called and qualified to do with a single eye to His glory and will, from a grateful sense of His love and mercy to us."[48] If anyone ever practiced that kind of religion, Wilberforce certainly did.

In time, Wilberforce was propelled to the forefront of the evangelical reform movement. In fact, he became known as its lay leader.[49] In true evangelical style, he proclaimed unabashedly that "Christianity calls her professors to a state of diligent watchfulness and active services."[50]

Wilberforce brought these views to bear in teaching his children what a real Christian life should be. In stark contrast to a society and church in which most were spiritually apathetic, he envisioned a faith that informed every aspect of life. He desperately wanted his children to understand that

[t]here are no indifferent actions properly speaking. I should rather say none with which religion has nothing to do. This however is the commonly received doctrine of those who consider themselves as very good Christians.... On the contrary, a true Christian holds in obedience to the injunction "Whatever you do in word or deed"... that the desire to please his God and Savior must be universal.... [T]he difference between real and nominal Christians is more manifest on small occasions than on greater. In the latter all who do not disclaim the authority of Christ's command must obey them – but in the former, only they will apply them who do make religion their grand business.

O, my very dear Samuel, be not satisfied with the name of Christian. But strive to be a Christian in life and in power and in the Holy Ghost.

Be at your post. Do on the day, the duties of the day, associating as much as you can the idea of pleasing Him whose you are and whom you serve.

It should be the grand object of our lives to form an inward state of heart and affections after the model of Christianity. If we watch ourselves and observe the operations of our own hearts, we shall discover the motive that naturally presents itself – whether it be the desire of approving ourselves to our fellow creatures or of approving ourselves to our God and Savior.

I scarcely need to remark to you that a people observing the same course of outward conduct and therefore appearing to men much the same, may to God appear quite different. And such as we appear to God, such we are, and shall be declared to be at the last day.

Persons who really deserve the honored name of Christians sometimes do not enough bear in mind the importance of associating the idea of their Savior with the lesser occasions of life as well as the greater. The greater of course seldom occur. But the smaller are continually presenting themselves and are therefore as often furnishing the means of forming a habit of recollecting the Savior on all occasions – in short, a habit of spiritual-mindedness. In truth this constitutes one of the chief distinctions between nominal and real Christians.

I will remind you of an idea which I threw out I believe on the day preceding your departure – that I feared I had scarcely enough endeavored to impress on my children – the idea that they must, as Christians, be a peculiar people. I am persuaded you cannot misunderstand me to mean that I wish you to affect singularities in indifferent matters. The very contrary is our duty. So far from being needlessly singular, we never ought to be so but for some special and good reason. But from that very circumstance of its being right that we should be like the rest of the world in exterior manners results an augmentation of the danger of our not maintaining that contrast which the eye of God ought to see in us to

139

the worldly way of thinking and feeling on all the various occasions of life and in relation to its various interests. For while by the world these are almost always viewed with reference to the invisible and eternal world, it is in that very relation that a Christian endeavors constantly to regard them. The man of the world considers religion as having nothing to do with 99/100ths of the affairs of life, considering it as a medicine and not as his food. Least of all as his refreshment and cordial. He naturally takes no more of it than his health requires. How opposite this to the apostle's admonition whatever ye do in word or deed, do all in the name of the Lord Jesus, giving thanks to God and the Father through Him. This is being spiritually minded, and being so is truly declared to be life and peace.

This teaching Wilberforce modeled well for his children. Beloved by English society, he nevertheless maintained Christian distinctives. As one of his friends once noted, if Wilberforce were less hospitable, "his children would see less of what may be most useful to them in his example. They would have less of that important and difficult lesson, how to live with the world, and yet not be of the world. They would be less likely to learn how to have their conversation in heaven, without renouncing the society of man; how to be cheerful in company, and to please both friends and strangers, without any sacrifice of Christian character."

Wilberforce's sentiments are perhaps best summarized in a prayer he recorded in his journal in 1801:

O God, give me a single heart and a single eye, fixed on Thy favours, and resolutely determined to live to Thy glory, careless whether I succeed or not in worldly concerns, leaving all my human interests and objects to Thee, and beseeching Thee to enable me to set my affections on things above; and walking by faith, to wait on Christ, and live on Him day by day here, till at length, through His infinite and wholly unmerited mercy, I am taken to dwell with Him hereafter in everlasting happiness and glory.[51]

In a similar spirit he wrote to one of his sons:

I wish I could be a less unprofitable servant. Yet I must remember Milton's sonnet, "They also serve who only stand and wait." Let us all be found in our several stations doing therein the Lord's work diligently and zealously.

Wilberforce was convinced that Christians bore a considerable responsibility and would one day be held accountable for the manner in which they lived out their faith. He did not consign his beliefs to one part of his mind or allow them to play out only in a particular subset of his actions. His beliefs informed every part of his life. He wrote to his children,

May you be enabled more and more to walk by faith, not by sight, to feel habitually as well as to recognize in all your more deliberate calculations and plans that the things that are seen are temporal but the things that are not seen are eternal. Thus you will live about

141

the world as one who is waiting for the coming of the Lord Jesus Christ.

Affectionately yours,
W. Wilberforce

Epilogue

Ever faithful to his beloved children, Wilberforce blessed them with heartfelt, wise, challenging letters to the end of his life. In the month of his death, July 1833, barely able to grasp a quill pen and with scarcely sufficient eyesight to write, he urged them on toward greater love and service for the Lord.

Wilberforce's lifelong, comprehensive approach to parenting was amply rewarded. In his later years, he was blessed with the opportunity to witness his children's obvious spiritual maturity as they began marriages, pursued meaningful careers, and embarked on their own journeys of parenthood. Wilberforce loved his children, their spouses, and his grandchildren tremendously. He considered his family to be his crowning achievement, or perhaps better expressed, the jewels in his crown. He often recounted in awe how God had blessed him through his wife and children. Over and over, particularly toward the end of his life, he would claim David's words for himself: "Surely goodness and mercy have followed me all the days of my life."

His children and their spouses lovingly cared for him during the last few years of his life while he and Barbara moved about, staying with one child and then another. Both Wilberforce and his wife relished this unique time to observe and enjoy their adult children and young grandchildren.

Their oldest child, William, was the only family member who engendered any family strife, and it was largely limited to financial matters. He became a businessman and unfortunately lost the Wilberforce family wealth on a bad investment. William was happily married, though, and seemed to have an otherwise stable family life.

Daughter Barbara, sadly, never had the opportunity to leave home and begin an independent life. She became ill with tuberculosis and died as a young adult in 1821.

Elizabeth, or Lizzy as her dad called her, was a voracious reader and married a clergyman of solid reputation. She served her husband's parishioners eagerly. Tragically, she became ill after giving birth to a healthy baby girl and died shortly thereafter.

Robert, Samuel, and Henry all studied at Oxford and became ministers, much to their father's delight. Wilberforce lived long enough to see that Robert and Samuel were happily married and enjoying the blessings of parenthood. Henry, still a student when his father passed away, later married as well. Samuel eventually became bishop of Oxford and was renowned in England in his own right.

With a domestic life marked by peace and joy, Wilberforce could relax in his last days. Trusting the Lord to act on his children's behalf as generously as He had on his own, he completed his race and passed the torch to the next generation.

Endnotes

1. George Barna, *Revolutionary Parenting* (Carol Stream, Il.: Tyndale House Publishers, Inc., 2007), 19.

2. quoted in Marvin Olasky, *The American Leadership Tradition: The Inevitable Impact of a Leader's Faith on a Nation's Destiny* (Wheaton, Ill.: Crossway Books, 1999), 111.

3. John Pollock, *Wilberforce* (New York: St. Martin's Press, 1977), 37-39, attributing Wilberforce's decision to remain in politics to Newton and Pitt.

4. Robert Isaac and Samuel Wilberforce, *The Life of William Wilberforce* (Freeport, N.Y.: Books for Libraries Press, 1972), 1:132, letter from John Newton to Wilberforce, July 21, 1796.

5. Ernest Marshall Howse, *Saints in Politics: The 'Clapham Sect' and the Growth of Freedom* (Toronto, University of Toronto Press, 1952), 16.

6. I have drawn many details about members of the Clapham Sect and their activities from E. M. Howse's *Saints in Politics*.

7. I Corinthians 15:33, NIV.

8. Ford K. Brown, *Fathers of the Evangelicals: The Age of Wilberforce* (Cambridge: Cambridge University Press, 1961), 42. Brown observes that a "striking aspect" of British society at this time was "the contrast between the immense wealth of the great and the degrading indigence and squalor of a large mass of the 'lower orders.'"

9. Howse, 5.

10. Brown, 42. George Macaulay Trevelyan, *British History in the Nineteenth Century* (London: Longmans, Green and Co., 1922),13.

11. Howse, 4.

12. Pollock, 139.

13. James 4:17, NIV.

14. *Life* 2:195, quoting a 1788 diary entry.

15. Philippians 1:21, NIV.

16. Pollock, 149.

17. *Life*, 1:126, letter to Lord Muncaster.

18. Philippians 1:9-11, NIV.

19. William Wilberforce, *Real Christianity*, abridged and updated by Ellyn Sanna (Uhrichsville, Ohio: Barbour Publishing, Inc., 1999), 18.

20. Kevin Charles Belmonte, ed., *A Practical View of Christianity* (Peabody, Mass.: Hendrickson Publishers, Inc., 1996), 71, n.2.

21. For a detailed account of the role Milner played in the conversion of Wilberforce, see Murray Andrew Pura, *Vital Christianity: The Life and Spirituality of William Wilberforce* (Toronto: Clements Publishing, 2002), 49-50. Also, see *Life*, 1:66-88.

22. For an excellent analysis of Puritan influence on Wilberforce's spirituality, see Pura, 92-101.

23. James Stephen, *Essays in Ecclesiastical Biography* (London: Longmans, Green, and Co., 1891), 483.

24. For a great discussion on this topic see Peter Kreeft, *Christianity for Modern Pagans: Pascal's Pensees Edited, Outlined, and Explained* (Ft. Collins, Co.: Ignatius Press, 1993).

25. Pollock, 163.

26. George Macaulay Trevelyan, *British History in the Nineteenth Century* (London: Longmans, Green and Co., 1922), 25.

27. Ibid., 29.

28. Ibid., 194.

29. *Life*, 2:129-30.

30. Jonathan Bayes, "William Wilberforce: His Impact on Nineteenth-Century Society," *Churchman* 108 (1994): 121, describing the Church of England as "lifeless" and the clergy as "lacking in spiritual fervor." Ian C. Bradley, *The Call to Seriousness: The Evangelical Impact on the Victorians* (New York: Macmillan, 1976), 59, noting that "the general caliber of Anglican clergymen was low."

31. Bradley, 59.

32. Bayes, 121.

33. Bradley, 59.

34. *Practical View*, 191.

35. *Life,* 2:63, November 1794, letter to Lord Muncaster.

36. *Practical View*

37. *Life*, vol. 2, Oct. 8, 1824, Appendix 401-3.

38. *Practical View*, 195.

39. Ibid., 194. Wilberforce wrote, "God is forgotten; his providence is exploded." Ibid., 196.

40. Ibid., 197.

41. Arthur Skevington Wood, "Wilberforce's Practical View," *Congregational Quarterly* 35 (1957): 253, 254.

42. quoted in Sir Reginald Coupland, *Wilberforce: A Narrative* (London: Collins, 1945), 199.

43. Anna Maria Wilberforce, ed., *The Private Papers of William Wilberforce* (London: T. Fisher Unwin, 1897), 40, letter from Wilberforce to William Pitt, postmarked Easter Sunday, 1797, noting that "the religion which I espouse differs practically from the common orthodox system."

44. Cowie, 55; Trevelyan, 25.

45. Bradley, 19.

46. Cowie, 55; Trevelyan, 25.

47. Bradley, 17.

48. Pura, 116, letter from John Newton to William Wilberforce, Dec. 13, 1794.

49. Bradley, 17; Trevelyan, 25.

50. Belmonte, 92.

51. *Life*, 3:23, journal entry from Dec. 20, 1801.